Sir Humphrey's Legacy

Facing Up to the Cost of Public Sector Pensions

D1334263

Sir Humphrey's Legacy

Facing Up to the Cost of
Public Sector Pensions

NEIL RECORD

WITH COMMENTARIES BY
PHILIP BOOTH
NICK SILVER

The Institute of Economic Affairs

First published in Great Britain in 2006 by
The Institute of Economic Affairs
2 Lord North Street
Westminster
London SW1P 3LB
in association with Profile Books Ltd

The mission of the Institute of Economic Affairs is to improve public
understanding of the fundamental institutions of a free society, by analysing and
explaining the role of markets in solving economic and social problems.

A CIP catalogue record for this book is available from the British Library.

ISBN-10: 0 255 36578 0
ISBN-13: 978 0 255 36578 9

Many IEA publications are translated into languages other than English or
are reprinted. Permission to translate or to reprint should be sought from the
Director General at the address above.

Typeset in Stone by Phoenix Photosetting, Chatham, Kent
www.phoenixphotosetting.co.uk

Printed and bound in Great Britain by Hobbs the Printers

CONTENTS

THE AUTHOR

Neil Record is chairman of Record Currency Management, a specialist currency manager. He was educated at Balliol College, Oxford, and University College London, from where he holds an MSc in Economics (with distinction). His first job was as an economist at the Bank of England; this was followed by a stint in industry. In 1983, he founded Record Currency Management. He has lectured on Investment Management at Cambridge University, and is author of the first book on specialist currency management within an institutional investment context: *Currency Overlay* (John Wiley & Sons, 2003). He is a member of the Investment Committee of Nuffield College, Oxford.

FOREWORD

The UK has recently experienced a major debate about the future of pensions policy. This debate has been informed by the analysis and recommendations of Lord Turner's independent Pensions Commission.

Though Lord Turner's remit was focused on private pension provision, the work of his commission soon expanded to consider the state pension system, and its impact on private saving. Lord Turner's report has been followed (May 2006) by a government White Paper on pensions which is likely to have major implications for the state pension architecture, for future retirement ages and for private pension saving.

In this great debate about pensions policy, however, one area has been seriously neglected – the consideration of public sector occupational pension reform. This monograph is a welcome and timely contribution to the pensions debate, and will help to move the focus on to this neglected but crucial area.

Public sector pensions are costly to provide, and this cost is poorly understood. There can be little doubt, however, that the cost burden is growing and that across the economy as a whole 'the present level of pension right accrual is … increasingly unequal' (Pensions Commission, 2005: 39).

There is an urgent public policy requirement to establish what the cost burden is likely to be, whether this is affordable, and whether reforms to public sector pensions are now needed to ensure that the burden on future taxpayers is bearable and fair.

Neil Record's estimates demonstrate that the cost of public sector pensions is growing, and he has derived the highest estimate yet for the unfunded liability of public sector schemes – at £1,025 billion. As the author himself acknowledges, these huge numbers are in and of themselves not immediately and intuitively meaningful, as it is possible for the government to accumulate large unfunded liabilities which are both affordable and sustainable.

It is Neil Record's other calculations which are of greater concern, because they cast doubt on the existing estimated costs of public sector pension schemes. Many schemes already seem to require very high levels of employer (i.e. taxpayer) contribution, based on existing government figures. These levels of employer contribution are often as much as twice the level of the best private sector schemes, and this raises concerns as to whether the private sector is having to pay unfairly to finance unreasonably generous public sector schemes (including the scheme for Members of Parliament!). But if Neil Record's figures are accurate, then the real cost of public sector schemes could be even higher, in which case the argument for reform will be even more pressing.

It is to be hoped that this monograph will stimulate others to join the debate, so that there can be a broadly agreed understanding of the costs of public sector pension provision, as the necessary precursor for a wider political debate about the options for reform.

My own view is that the government should establish an independent commission on the lines of Lord Turner's recent model, to establish a consensus on the costs of public sector pensions, and to set out clear recommendations for reform.

Reform options must include a review of retirement ages, accrual rates, final salary and career-averaging arrangements, employer and employee contribution rates, defined-contribution options, and the accounting for and funding of schemes.

The government's own recent efforts to reform public sector pensions have been modest in scope and misguided in detail. In particular, it is ironic, and likely to be unpopular with many in the private sector, that all existing public sector employees in many of the biggest schemes will be allowed to continue to retire at age 60, up until around 2045. This contrasts with the government's decision to raise the age at which the basic state pension will be received from 65 to 68, starting as early as 2024.

It is also ironic that the Chancellor of the Exchequer has been so determined to keep down the cost of the state pension and that we are to continue with the existing, complex and mass means-tested system for many decades, yet public sector pension costs are likely to rise by around 50 per cent as a share of the economy over the next few decades.

The challenge for the future is not simply to level down all non-state pension provision to the lowest common denominator – public sector pension costs must be affordable, and the balance between taxpayers and employees must be fair.

The figures in this IEA monograph suggest that existing public sector pension arrangements may be neither fair nor affordable. This is a valuable contribution to a debate that can no longer be postponed.

DAVID LAWS, MP
June 2006

ACKNOWLEDGEMENTS

I have received help in preparing this monograph from a number of individuals and organisations. I would like to mention in particular the Government Actuary's Department for answering my letters clearly and fully, and for pointing me in the direction of source material; Stephen Yeo of Watson Wyatt for helpful and supportive comments on an earlier draft; Brian St J. Hall of Hewitt Associates for helpful suggestions on actuarial and demographic assumptions; Nick Silver for very full and constructive comments on an earlier draft; my colleague Ian Harrison for his sharp-eyed proofreading; and Philip Dunne, MP, David Willetts, MP, and David Laws, MP (the author of the Foreword) for their reinforcement of my belief that the effort and care I have taken in studying this area will not be ignored by policy-makers.

The IEA is very grateful for the support of the charity CHK for this project.

SUMMARY

- Official estimates of public sector pension liabilities do not use sound accounting or actuarial methodology and, as such, they woefully underestimate the true liability that taxpayers owe to public sector workers in the form of future pensions.
- Private sector pension schemes now have to disclose their pension liabilities transparently. As shareholders increasingly understand the costs of final salary, defined-benefit pension schemes, companies are taking action to reduce costs by closing those schemes. In the public sector, the costs are still hidden and the incentives for action to be taken to reduce costs are limited.
- While the official government estimate of public sector pension liabilities is £530 billion, an estimate using more realistic assumptions than the government uses would be £1,025 billion. This sum is over 80 per cent of GDP and over twice the size of the official national debt. These commitments must be honoured by government, and thus pension liabilities should be regarded in the same way as the official national debt. Little can be done about the size of liabilities accumulated to date.
- The government can take action to stop the liability growing. Each year, it makes £41 billion of new pension commitments

to its employees. Furthermore, public sector pay increases not only make future pension promises more expensive, they also add to the cost of meeting past pension promises because these were defined in terms of an employee's salary at retirement.

- The annual cost of public sector pension promises already made will peak at nearly £90 billion in 2045. People who are currently too young to vote will bear the greatest burden.
- When calculated correctly, the cost of pensions in the public sector varies from 35 per cent of salary for male teachers to 72 per cent of salary for policewomen. Public sector employers are charged much less than this.
- Governance in public sector pension schemes is very weak, leading to extremely high ill-health retirement rates – for example, 39 per cent for local government employees and 68 per cent for fire service employees.
- Government reforms of public sector pensions have been trivial and have not addressed the underlying problems.
- When public sector pension promises are made, they should be costed explicitly and properly funded using index-linked gilts.
- The government should charge public sector employers (NHS trusts, schools, police authorities, etc.) the full cost of providing their employees' pensions. Employers would then be free to negotiate with employees new pay packages that involved less pension provision and higher salaries. Public sector employees may well welcome this.

TABLES, FIGURES AND BOXES

AUTHOR'S PREFACE: THE TRUE COST OF PUBLIC SECTOR PENSIONS

The combined unfunded public sector pension schemes in the UK now have a very substantial call on the nation's future taxes and taxpayers. This paper attempts to analyse this liability from two perspectives: first, the total value of the pension obligations under the current rules, and second, the 'real' current cost expressed as a percentage of salary in each of the large public sector employers. By 'real' cost, I mean the amount of money that would have to be put aside each year to fully fund the future pension cost without any investment risk being taken by the government.

My estimate of the 'headline' unfunded public sector occupational pensions liability at March 2006 is £1,025 billion, or 83 per cent of GDP. This is £495 billion higher than the last official estimate (£530 billion) for March 2005 and £65 billion higher than the latest Watson Wyatt estimate (£960 billion) for March 2006.

My estimates of the annual costs as a percentage of salary are shown in detail in Chapter 3, but as an example, whereas in the case of the teachers' scheme the government charges employees 6 per cent of salary, and employers (Local Education Authorities) 13.5 per cent of salary (i.e. a total cost of 19.5 per cent), I calculate that the total 'real' annual cost of teachers' pensions is 34.7 per cent of salary for men and 39.0 per cent for women.

This monograph calculates pension liabilities on current scheme rules. The government and the main public sector unions have been in negotiation over reform of the schemes (prompted by the government), to make them more affordable. The current compromise proposal is to raise the normal retirement age to 65 for new employees, but not for existing employees. This will not alter the current headline liability figure, nor (obviously) the 'real cost' calculations for existing employees. It will reduce the real cost of pensions for new employees, and this is quantified in Chapter 3.

I set out the basic facts of the main public sector schemes in Chapter 1. I attempt to analyse the 'pensions promise' from first principles in Chapter 2. In Chapter 3, I translate the theory into estimates of the liability and the 'real' pensions running costs from the most up-to-date numbers in government publications. Finally, in Chapter 4, I briefly review the policy alternatives to address the problem.[1]

My main aim has been to ensure that these costs are made transparent because it is impossible to have a constructive policy debate in the absence of a proper understanding of the costs of alternatives. My proposals in Chapter 4 and the proposals of the commentators, Philip Booth and Nick Silver, are intended to start a more radical policy debate in the context of the work to uncover the real costs of public sector pensions.

---

1   The timing of the information used in the monograph is as follows. The information used in Chapter 1 is accurate as at October 2005; Chapter 2 is written against a background of real interest rates as at March 2005 (c. 1.6 per cent p.a.), although since it is a description of principles, the real rate is used only for stylised examples; Chapter 3 has been updated for interest rates prevailing as at March 2006 (c. 1.1 per cent p.a.). Chapter 4 summarises the government's financial position as at March 2006.

Sir Humphrey's Legacy

Facing Up to the Cost of Public Sector Pensions

1 EXISTING UNFUNDED PUBLIC SERVICE PENSION SCHEMES

Introduction

According to the Office for National Statistics (ONS), in March 2004, the latest period available, 5.7 million people were employed in the public sector, compared with total UK employment of 28.3 million – so 20 per cent of all UK employment is in the public sector. Interestingly, when asked who they work for, some 6.9 million people (or 24 per cent) say they work for the public sector.[1] This discrepancy arises from the definitions of public and private sector: definitions that are surprisingly difficult to pin down. For example, most university employees will say that they work in the public sector. On UK National Accounts definitions, however, universities are in the private sector, not the public sector. So the 5.7 million refers to National Accounts definitions, not what people generally think of as public sector.[2]

Most employees in the public sector are offered a final salary pension scheme. There are six large employers' pension schemes which account for the vast majority of the occupational pension

---

1   Source: Office for National Statistics (ONS) Labour Force Survey (LFS).

2   Non-intuitive examples of public sector employers include Channel 4 Television Corporation Ltd and Hillingdon Homes Ltd (both of which are classified as public corporations and therefore in the public sector), whereas National Air Traffic Services Ltd, a subsidiary of the Civil Aviation Authority, is classified as a private sector employer.

obligations of the government, five of which are unfunded, and one of which (the Local Government Pension Scheme) is funded. The full list of unfunded schemes is shown in Appendix 1 (the main five are in bold).[3]

All these schemes have pension obligations to their members that are not backed in any way by marketable assets (or indeed segregated assets of any kind). They rely wholly on the covenant of the UK government.

Are unfunded pension schemes a bad idea ?

Is there anything inherently wrong in unfunded pension schemes in the public sector? Probably not. The arguments for funding public sector pensions per se are not strong. The main purpose of funding, after all, is to ensure that pensioners get paid, and the one employer who is certain to continue to be solvent, and to be able to fulfil its promises to pensioners, is the government. Its tax-raising powers make this a near-certainty,[4] rather than just highly probable.

The problem with unfunded public sector schemes is not lack of security for members. It is instead that (i) commitments made by one generation have to be paid for by subsequent generations (rather than paid for at the time of commitment) and (ii) the scale of the commitments may not be subject to scrutiny of the same rigour as that which applies to the funded pensions sector.

---

3 Note that Scotland and Northern Ireland sometimes, but not always, have their own schemes.

4 *In extremis* (say a revolution) the *will* to pay might disappear – but we will stick in this paper with the idea that the UK government has no credit risk attached to its promises.

Point (i) is a general problem of unfunded pensions, which most European countries (including the UK) are facing in their state pension arrangements. Much has been written about it, and I do not propose to add to that debate.

On point (ii), the funded sector, which was originally designed to put aside enough money each year to cover all pension liabilities, has had its own, much-publicised, problems. The answer to the question 'how large a fund do we need to cover our liabilities?' has been twisted slowly and subtly over time by a combination of wishful thinking, misaligned incentives, short-termism and client accommodation by actuaries. The government, in its role as pensions regulator, did little until recently to stem this tide. The result was the 'pensions black hole', the approximately £100 billion gap between the pension liabilities (measured by the FRS17[5] standard) of the FTSE 100 companies and the size of their pension funds.[6] Market pressures apply to private pension schemes, however, in a way that they do not to public sector schemes. The advent of the FRS17 measure, and in particular in the UK the Pension Protection Fund, are evidence that reality can

---

5   FRS17 is a new accounting standard which requires UK companies to value their pensions liabilities using a discount rate equal to the yield on AA corporate bonds. While this is not as stringent as either using a gilts discount rate or a rate of interest that would reflect the cost of the fund having its liabilities insured, it is much better than the now discredited Minimum Funding Requirement (MFR). A new international standard, IAS19, looks very like FRS17. In the past it has been possible for defined-benefit pension benefits to be adjusted so that scheme members took some of the risk of under-funding. Legislation has closed off some of these 'safety valves', thus whatever the merits of techniques used in the past, in the current environment defined-benefit pension promises should be treated as promises and liabilities valued accordingly.

6   This was the size of the gap at its peak – it is now (April 2006) lower, but highly variable.

be avoided only for so long – in the long run it invariably makes itself felt.

Without clear knowledge of the cost, no sensible decisions can be made by either party – employer or employee – as to the right level of pensions (i.e. deferred pay) as compared with salary level (paid now).

For the unfunded public sector, in place of accurate calculations of the real costs of pensions, as we shall see, is a series of 'non-market' assumptions which distort the cost calculation, and therefore the decision-making process.

Some of the UK's public sector pension schemes use a model called SCAPE,[7] in which a notional fund is maintained for each scheme, with 'contributions' invested (notionally, of course) in index-linked gilts.[8] On the basis of the assumptions in each scheme, the amount of contributions by employees and employers is required to be adequate, over time, to provide sufficient notional funds under SCAPE to cover the liabilities. The 'notional' nature of SCAPE, however, has allowed (notional) investment in index-linked gilts at yields far higher than are available in the market, lowering the apparent cost of the pensions. We will come back to this point in much more detail later.

---

7   Superannuation Contributions Adjusted for Past Experience. This is a good idea (using actuarial maths to calculate accurate annual pensions costs to each public sector employer) but spoiled by the use of an artificial discount rate.

8   Bonds issued by the UK government (gilts) generally pay a fixed rate of interest (coupon) twice a year until they mature, when the government pays the capital back in full. Index-linked gilts do exactly the same, but both the capital and the interest are uprated each month in line with the (eight-month-lagged) RPI. This preserves their purchasing power. The Debt Management Office, which issues gilts on behalf of the government, has changed the indexation rules for new index-linked bonds, but the greater part of the market follows the eight-month time-lag rule.

Facts about each scheme

Table 1 is a summary of the main unfunded public sector pension schemes. I have not included smaller schemes, and those listed below account for some 95 per cent of the outstanding unfunded liabilities.

There are other pension schemes (all funded to a greater or lesser extent) that are also the responsibility of the taxpayer – examples are the Local Government Pension Scheme (LGPS), the universities, Royal Mail, the BBC, the Bank of England, and partial guarantees to many former nationalised industries such as coal, railways and, as we discovered in April 2006, BT. I do not intend, however, to refer to these any further in this paper, although it would be an interesting topic for another paper. Suffice it to say that in teasing out unfunded government pension liabilities, we will not have got to the bottom of the total pension liabilities to which the taxpayer is ultimately committed.

Table 1 **Main unfunded public sector pension schemes**

Employer	Coverage	Normal retirement age	Accrual rate[9]	Lump sum[10]	Widows/ dependants[11]
Teachers	England & Wales	60	$\frac{1}{80}$th	3x	50%
NHS	England & Wales	60	$\frac{1}{80}$th	3x	50%
Civil	UK – pre-2002	60	$\frac{1}{80}$th	3x	50%
Service	UK – post-2002	60	$\frac{1}{60}$th	Nil[12]	37.5%
Police	GB	55	0–20 yrs – $\frac{1}{60}$th 20+ yrs – $\frac{1}{30}$th Max. $\frac{2}{3}$ salary	Nil[13]	50%
Armed forces	UK – pre-2005	55	0–16 yrs – $\frac{1}{56}$th 16+ yrs – $\frac{1}{90}$th	3x	50%
	UK – post-2005	55	$\frac{1}{70}$th	3x	62.5%

Accrual accounting and the difficulties in defining the true cost of pensions

Calculating the true cost of pension liabilities is surprisingly difficult, for a number of reasons. The first is that the government traditionally accounts on a 'cash' basis, rather than an accruals[14] basis. Unfunded pensions are by their nature an 'accruals' item as no cash is spent by the government as workers accrue pension rights (the cash payments come much later). In recent years, however, the government has begun to apply accruals accounting to some areas, and this has helped with finding some of the numbers needed. The second difficulty is that the 'public sector' is not one employer, and that the pension arrangements, and the assumptions that underpin their pension accounts, differ across employers. The third difficulty is that, despite the scale of the public spending that these pension schemes absorb, the amount of published information on them is slight, and what there is requires considerable expertise and diligence to find.

The final difficulty is that the very long horizons of pension liabilities, and the statistical elements within them, make understanding very difficult for lay people. To unravel this complexity

9   This refers to the proportion of final salary that is accrued as pension with each year's service.

10   This refers to the multiple of pension paid as a tax-free lump sum.

11   This refers to the proportion of pension paid to the widow/widower of a pensioner who dies while drawing his pension.

12   Part of the pension can be commuted to a lump sum.

13   Part of the pension can be commuted to a lump sum.

14   In simple terms, 'cash' basis is the amount of cash spent or received in a year, irrespective of what good or service it is payment for, or the date of delivery or consumption of that good or service. 'Accruals' basis, by contrast, measures only the goods and services consumed in the year, whatever the terms or timing of payment. The accruals basis is a much better measure of the economic picture year by year, although in the (very) long run 'cash' and 'accruals' will coincide.

has required the expertise of actuaries. For several reasons, this has allowed the creation and maintenance of a 'mystique' around liability valuation that has become their almost exclusive preserve.

Without the full employment records of some 5 million employees, the task of valuing from first principles the pensions liabilities owed by a series of public sector employers is impossible. I therefore plan to adopt the following approach to reduce the task to manageable proportions.

Calculation of outstanding liabilities
- I will use a 'methodology' section in the monograph to establish, from first principles, the financial mathematics of pension liabilities. This will be presented without assuming any actuarial expertise on behalf of the reader.
- The valuation of scheme liabilities within the public domain as provided by the Government Actuary's Department (GAD) and other official sources will be used.
- The assumptions underlying these estimates will be examined and I will select a small number of critical assumptions which have a disproportionate effect on liability valuations.
- I will establish realistic values for each of these assumptions (many may already be realistic) and then examine the likely effect of these new assumption values on the liabilities using the financial mathematics methodology.

Calculation of ongoing pension cost
- I will use financial mathematics to estimate the current cost of

pensions (expressed as a percentage of salary) at an aggregate level based on the new assumptions.
- This will be compared with the 'cost of pensions' calculated by GAD, which is in the public domain.
- The policy implications of the 'real' cost of pensions compared with 'official' costs will then be considered.

While there is no doubt that an important result of these calculations will be the figure for the overall scale of the government's unfunded liability, this value is not of great importance from a policy perspective. Existing liabilities are just that – little can be done to reduce them short of expropriation[15] – whereas each day that passes, public sector employers are paying public sector employees large amounts of deferred pay in the form of new pensions promises, while having a mistaken idea about how much these amounts are. Good decision-making on the part of both employers and employees needs, at minimum, basic facts (such as a knowledge of the monetary value of the salary and the benefits package) to be clear. The main aim of this monograph is to improve this clarity.

---

15 A form of which would be raising the retirement age for existing employees in respect of benefits already accrued.

2 METHODOLOGY OF CALCULATING A PENSION LIABILITY

Introduction

Any employer who offers a 'defined-benefit'[1] pension to any employee is making a promise to pay, in effect, part of the pay package in arrears. So much in arrears, in fact, that it is paid after the employee has retired – which could be 80 years[2] or more after the 'pay' was earned. The promise commits the employer to pay a defined amount *each year* as long as the retired employee lives.

Government pension promises are unfunded – except for local authorities

Generally speaking, as we have seen, the government has taken the line that it does not have to fund pensions in advance (i.e. create pension funds) because it will not go bankrupt. There is one exception to this – the Local Government Pension Scheme (LGPS), which is funded, and covers local authority employees not in other (unfunded) schemes such as police officers and teachers.

---

1   In the UK almost all defined-benefit schemes are 'final salary'-based – hence the popularity of the expression. This naming convention may change if a significant proportion of schemes try to renegotiate to average salary arrangements.

2   In the case of a twenty-year-old's 'deferred pay' still being paid (in the form of pension) when he (or more likely she) celebrates her hundredth birthday.

When an employer such as the government undertakes to pay a pension, it takes on a debt.[3] The government takes on future obligations in a number of ways, not all of which are classified by the government as debt, but much of which is. The most explicit debts are gilts and Treasury bills – which together with National Savings obligations make up the vast bulk of what is colloquially know as the 'national debt'. Some other types of debt – namely commitments under PFI and occupational pensions – are not officially classified as debt, even though they may be.[4]

There are many other types of future expenditure to which the government is committed (state pensions, education, health, the military – indeed, virtually all categories of public sector provision), but these are political, not contractual, obligations. No one could have taken the government to court for indexing state pensions to the Retail Price Index (RPI), not earnings, or could do so for making cuts in health provision – whereas an employee could, in theory, take his public sector employer to court for reneging on the terms of the pension scheme and to which he may have been contributing.

There is a nicer point here, too. Governments can often avoid legal obligations by changing the law. The point is not particularly the legal enforceability of a particular commitment, but the consequences to government of default. The UK government has always paid its gilts commitments on time and in full because it wants to offer future investors an unblemished record, and thereby raise

---

3   There is a lot of rather mealy-mouthed semantics in this area. I will treat 'promise', 'debt', 'liability', 'commitment', etc., as all being synonymous – a contractual commitment by an employer to pay an employee the pension as defined in the scheme rules.

4   PFI commitments may, confusingly, be a combination of debt (deferred payment for current services or consideration) and future payment for future services.

funds on the finest terms. Similarly, the government, in the role of employer, is acting as an economic agent, not just as a political entity. It needs to compete with other, private sector, employers for the best staff at the best price. Reneging on its pension obligations would wreck its credibility as an employer, and compromise its ability to attract the staff it needs.

This monograph aims to highlight not just the size of the government's current occupational pension liability (about which little can be done short of default), but also the current cost of future pension arrangements (about which a great deal can be done). This latter concept is quite sophisticated, and much of this chapter is dedicated to explaining it.

Calculating liabilities[5]

If I am an employer, and I promise to pay you, my employee, £10,000 p.a. from retirement (say, when you are 60) until your death, how much do I owe you? Let's call this 'Promise 1'.

This simple enough question has provided a colourful debate over 50 years, occupying until only recently purely the actuarial profession, but more recently accountants, regulators, politicians, economists and lawyers. It is surprising that there has been a debate at all, since the theory has been fully in place since the eighteenth century,[6] and only some empirical data (mainly on longevity) has been significantly updated.

---

5   In this chapter I base most of the actual liability estimates on interest rates either in March 2005 or June 2005. In Chapter 3 I will use interest rates as at 31 March 2006. This chapter is designed simply to illustrate the concepts.

6   The truly diligent should see Haberman and Sibbett (1995).

Life expectancy in the UK has been rising for 150 years. Very roughly, it has increased by three months for every year that has passed in the last 150 years, so that if life expectancy at birth was 43 years in 1855, it is 80.5 years in 2005.

The pattern of death has changed a lot (there is much lower mortality among the very young), and this has meant that life expectancy of 60-year-olds has not increased anything like as much as the life expectancy of babies. There are a lot of complex concepts that actuaries like to wrap all the figures up in, but increases in life expectancy are not new, should be no surprise, and yet seem to have been continually surprising the profession. This has meant that life insurance has been over-priced and pensions or annuities have been under-priced.

An annuity is exactly 'Promise 1' above, offered not by an employer, but by a commercial provider (invariably an insurance company in the UK). It can be bought for cash, either on the day the employee is 60, or before the employee is 60 (it is then known as a 'deferred annuity'). It is priced in such a way that the provider will make a very small profit (a few per cent) if you live to exactly the planned life expectancy.[7]

Whether annuities are under-priced or not, the life insurance industry has managed to profit from selling annuity business. It has done so because it has been clear-headed about how (with the exception of the longevity trend point) to price and hedge annuities. To eliminate the longevity point, and to keep the calculation

---

7   This is not strictly true in mathematical terms. In fact the insurance company does not care about individuals in the same way that a good bookie does not mind about individual race outcomes. But the insurance company does care that the out-turn age at death of the population of customers matches the life expectancy curve on which it has priced the annuity.

simple in this example, I assume that life expectancy is 80 years, and that everyone dies at this age.[8]

Table 2 shows the calculation the insurance company undertakes to calculate the break-even price. Market interest rates in this example are 5 per cent (i.e. the insurance company can always invest at 5 per cent). In summary, if the insurance company charges £128,212 on the day the annuitant is 60, then it will invest this money at 5 per cent, and at each year-end add the interest earned in the year,[9] and deduct the £10,000 paid to the annuitant. By charging exactly £128,212 it will end up with precisely nothing when the annuitant dies at 80.[10] This is my definition of the 'fair price' for the annuity, and similarly is the amount that the annuity (or pension) provider 'owes' by making 'Promise 1'.

We can think of the relationship between the annual pension (£10,000) and the total liability for the provider (£128,212) as a ratio. £128,212/£10,000 = 12.8 (the 'annuity multiple'), or alternatively £10,000/£128,212 = 7.8 per cent ('annuity rate'). We will come back to these concepts later. Note that the total amount paid out (£210,000) is a lot more that the £128,212 needed to fully cover the liability – and this is all the effect of compound interest: the insurer can earn interest on the money that is set aside to accumulate to meet the annuity liability.

When set out like this, the calculation of the £128,212 looks a bit as if we reached it by trial and error. It is the right answer

---

8   Later on, in more accurate calculations, I will take into account the chance element in age at death, and its wide spread.

9   I assume that the annuity provider will not pay tax on this interest. This is generally true in the UK, and certainly true for pension funds.

10   In this example, the annuitant dies at midnight the day before his 81st birthday – so he gets the 80th year's cheque.

Table 2 **Simplified example annuity (£)**

Age	Amount invested at start of year	Plus interest	Less pension paid out	Total investment end year
60	128,212	6,411	− 10,000	124,622
61	124,622	6,231	− 10,000	120,853
62	120,853	6,043	− 10,000	116,896
63	116,896	5,845	− 10,000	112,741
64	112,741	5,637	− 10,000	108,378
65	108,378	5,419	− 10,000	103,797
66	103,797	5,190	− 10,000	98,986
67	98,986	4,949	− 10,000	93,936
68	93,936	4,697	− 10,000	88,633
69	88,633	4,432	− 10,000	83,064
70	83,064	4,153	− 10,000	77,217
71	77,217	3,861	− 10,000	71,078
72	71,078	3,554	− 10,000	64,632
73	64,632	3,232	− 10,000	57,864
74	57,864	2,893	− 10,000	50,757
75	50,757	2,538	− 10,000	43,295
76	43,295	2,165	− 10,000	35,460
77	35,460	1,773	− 10,000	27,232
78	27,232	1,362	− 10,000	18,594
79	18,594	930	− 10,000	9,524
80	9,524	476	− 10,000	0
Total paid out			210,000	

(since the amount left in the pot at aged 80 is zero), but it is not clear how we got there.

In fact, we can get there using the same principles but a different technique, which financial mathematicians call 'discounting'. I will start by taking the simplest possible example. I owe you £100 in exactly one year's time – how much do I owe you now? Or, how much could I pay you now instead of £100 in one year? The answer to this question is the amount that we need to invest at the rate of interest to produce our £100 in one year. We can apply the same investment technique as above (i.e. invest an amount of money at 5 per cent, which when added to the original amount will equal £100 in one year's time), but this time we can write out a simple equation to discover how much we need now:

(1) $A \times (1+r) = 100$

where A is the amount of money needed now, and r is the interest rate.

We can rearrange the equation to find A:

(2) $A = 100/(1+r)$

Since r = 5 per cent, then A = 100/1.05, or 95.24.

This value of A – 95.24 – is the present value (PV) of the debt discounted at 5 per cent, and is a crucial concept in pensions. The present value is the amount of money I need to invest now to fully pay all the amounts I owe in the future.[11]

Present values can apply to multi-year distant liabilities. Let us suppose I owe you the money in two years' time, rather than one. Assume that the interest I earn on my deposit arrives at the end of the year in one lump, and that I can reinvest the interest to earn interest on interest in the second year.[12] Then A (I will now call it PV) can be calculated in the following equation:

(3) $((PV \times (1+r^{*})) \times (1+r^{**})) = 100$
* interest year 1
** interest year 2

---

11 It also applies symmetrically to assets. If you (or perhaps the government) owe me a fixed amount of money at a future date, then the present value is what it is worth now, and in theory what I could sell it for to a third party if I needed the money now.

12 Again, this assumes no tax to pay on the interest: this is not generally true for individuals, but it is true for pension providers.

where PV is the present value.

Simplifying:

(4) $PV \times (1+r)^2 = 100$, so

(5) $PV = 100/(1+r)^2$

In fact we can make a general statement that any amount of money owed in n years' time has a present value as follows:

(6) $PV = 100/(1+r)^n$

Table 3 **Present value of a simplified pension (£)**

Age	Pension paid out	Present value of each payment
60	– 10,000	– 9,524
61	– 10,000	– 9,070
62	– 10,000	– 8,638
63	– 10,000	– 8,227
64	– 10,000	– 7,835
65	– 10,000	– 7,462
66	– 10,000	– 7,107
67	– 10,000	– 6,768
68	– 10,000	– 6,446
69	– 10,000	– 6,139
70	– 10,000	– 5,847
71	– 10,000	– 5,568
72	– 10,000	– 5,303
73	– 10,000	– 5,051
74	– 10,000	– 4,810
75	– 10,000	– 4,581
76	– 10,000	– 4,363
77	– 10,000	– 4,155
78	– 10,000	– 3,957
79	– 10,000	– 3,769
80	– 10,000	– 3,589
Total paid	210,000	128,212

This allows us to use the present value calculation to value any amount owed for any date in the future. So we can recast Table 2 as Table 3, using the present value concept.

The amount of money an annuity provider needs to invest to meet all these 'pension' payments turns out to be the sum of the present values of all the individual payments. This sum is commonly called the net present value (or 'NPV'), and is *the* fundamental financial concept that we need to understand to be able to answer the question 'how much is a pension promise worth now?'

I mentioned that present values are calculated by 'discounting' future cash flows to today's values. I just note here, to revisit later, that the interest rate I have used (5 per cent in this example) is called the 'discount rate'.

Index linking

I am about to make the pension promise more complicated. Let us stay with our current mortality assumptions, but change the pension promise – I want to give an index-linked pension. An index-linked pension means a pension whose value rises each year in line with the RPI (i.e. inflation). So now, if the promise is an annual payment of £10,000 p.a. *index-linked* from retirement at 60 until your death, how much do I owe you? Let us call this 'Promise 2'.

Fortunately for us (and anyone who wants to calculate the PV of an index-linked pension), there is a lively market in index-linked government debt (or 'index-linked gilts'). The government can borrow money, and the general public invest it, at a fixed 'real' rate of return. The 'real' rate of return is the guaranteed return over and above changes in the RPI[13] (i.e. inflation). The real interest rate varies with the length of time for which the investor wants it fixed. On the basis of prices on 21 June 2005, you could invest money for four years at 1.68 per cent p.a.; for eleven years also at 1.68 per cent p.a.; for nineteen years at 1.61 per cent; and for 30 years at 1.49 per cent p.a.[14] These rates are not a guess – an investor can invest his money today and get these rates, unconditionally guaranteed in interest and principal by the UK government. These rates are not set by the government, they are set by the market. The price of index-linked gilts varies in the second-hand market (i.e. the stock market) according to supply and demand. Real interest rates can vary widely. Since 1981 (which is when index-linked gilts were first issued), real rates have varied both up and down in a range of approximately 1.1 per cent to 4.5 per cent p.a.: so current real rates are at or near the lows of the past twenty years.

With index-linked gilts we can answer the question of how much Promise 2 is worth today. Sidestepping a few technicalities,

13 Note that the government has recently created an unresolved confusion about what constitutes inflation. For the purposes of index-linked gilts, public sector occupational pension schemes and the state pension, inflation is still measured by the Retail Price Index (RPI), and pensions and gilts are uprated in line with the RPI. The Bank of England, however, now targets a measure called the Consumer Price Index (CPI), which is calculated on a different basis, and has had a fifteen-year history of its annual rate of increase being around 0.85 per cent p.a. lower than RPI. There is pressure (from the point of view of both consistency and the government saving money) to change pensions and gilts to CPI linking, but this change is likely to be strongly resisted (with good reason) by the two affected groups – pensioners and investors. Any change of name of the current CPI to RPI should ring alarm bells.

14 In September 2005, the government issued an index-linked gilt with the longest maturity ever, maturing in 2055. It was issued by competitive tender, and was priced on issue at a real return of just 1.11 per cent p.a. real!

Table 4 **Present value of an index-linked simplified pension (£)**

Age	Pension paid out	Present value of each payment
60	– 10,000	– 9,842
61	– 10,000	– 9,686
62	– 10,000	– 9,532
63	– 10,000	– 9,381
64	– 10,000	– 9,232
65	– 10,000	– 9,086
66	– 10,000	– 8,942
67	– 10,000	– 8,801
68	– 10,000	– 8,661
69	– 10,000	– 8,524
70	– 10,000	– 8,389
71	– 10,000	– 8,256
72	– 10,000	– 8,125
73	– 10,000	– 7,996
74	– 10,000	– 7,870
75	– 10,000	– 7,745
76	– 10,000	– 7,622
77	– 10,000	– 7,501
78	– 10,000	– 7,383
79	– 10,000	– 7,266
80	– 10,000	– 7,150
Total paid	210,000	176,990

we can simply apply the current real rate of return (say 1.61 per cent – the nineteen years rate) to Table 2. Table 4 illustrates this. Note that I have not increased any of the payments by inflation – they are all still £10,000. But I don't have to – investing in index-linked gilts means that everything I own (i.e. principal and interest) will rise exactly in line with inflation. So I don't have to guess inflation, but I can still make the promise to index-link the £10,000, and be able to satisfy it with certainty. In other words, all the amounts in the table are in constant purchasing power terms ('real' terms) and the rate of interest used to calculate the present value is a 'real' rate over and above inflation.

So the answer to the question of how much Promise 2 is worth is £176,990. This is an annuity multiple of 17.7, and an annuity rate of 5.6 per cent.

The simple act of index linking has had a dramatic upward effect on the NPV of the liabilities. But the 5 per cent p.a. assumption was not the market interest rate – it was just a round-number assumption. On 21 June 2005, the conventional gilt yield for a twenty-year bond was 4.36 per cent. A 4.36 per cent interest rate gives an NPV of £135,753. So by index linking a pension, we increase the current liability by 30 per cent. But this is only half the story, as we shall see in a moment when we come to the 'final salary' section.

Mortality

Life expectancy in the UK is rising; it has been rising for a century and a half, and it is still rising. Life expectancy is simply an estimate of future death rates in the population, by age, based on past trends. Forecasting mortality requires that we make certain assumptions. These will not be totally arbitrary (since we have a lot of data on past mortality rates), but, just to illustrate the problem, with regard to future changes in mortality, do we assume that death rates at each age remain constant? That the rate of fall in the death rates at each age remains constant? Or that the change in the rate of fall in the death rates remains constant? Or do we base the forecasts on cohorts that experience particular mortality rates? And if none of these values has been constant in the past, what do we rely on? We will come back to this problem in Chapter 3.

The Government Actuary's Department (GAD) produces

cohort tables,[15] which aim to extrapolate established mortality trends across cohorts.[16] Just to put some numbers on this theory, Figure 1 shows the life expectancy projections at age 60 based on the UK cohort tables, prepared by GAD.

The cohort information above assumes a continuation of reducing mortality rates, but also needs a different mortality table for each year's cohort. For the purposes of illustration, this is far too complicated. I therefore propose to use the GAD's 2001–03

Figure 1   **Projected life expectancy at 60**

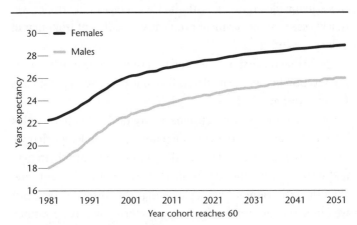

Source: GAD 2003, interim tables for UK

---

15   Cohort life expectancy at age 65 in 2000 would be worked out using the mortality rate for age 65 in 2000, for age 66 in 2001, for age 67 in 2002, and so on. Obviously, in cohort life tables we run out of actual data in this example after 2004. If, however, there have been consistent trends, these projections are likely to be closer to the future outcomes than just using constant death rates (called period tables).

16   In this context a cohort is all the people born in a particular year.

interim period[17] tables to calculate the life expectancy; we will just accept that it will almost certainly underestimate longevity – under these tables males aged 60 have a life expectancy of twenty further years, and females 23 further years.

Using this data, I will make a new pensions promise and calculate its PV. This is 'I promise to pay you (Mr and Mrs Average respectively) an index-linked pension of £10,000 p.a. from your 60th birthday until you die'.

Table 5 shows the amount payable each year (and again I do not increase the payment by inflation) if the pensioners of this scheme die off in line with the UK averages. The reader will quickly see that the payment profile is very different from that of Tables 2, 3 and 4.

Note that the first payment (on the last day of their 61st year) is not £10,000 because a small (less than one per cent) of pensioners will already have died.

All the public sector pensions we are dealing with are index linked. We can apply the same discounting methodology that we discussed earlier to calculate an NPV of this liability for both men and women, using the current market real return discount rate. We obviously cannot have a single maturity discount rate, but we can use an approximation of the maturity by mixing various maturity rates – 75 per cent of the nineteen-year rate (1.61 per

17   Period tables calculate, for example, life expectancy at age 65 in 2000 using the mortality rate for age 65 in 2000, for age 66 in 2000, for age 67 in 2000, and so on. They have two weaknesses: they do not allow for future improvements in mortality beyond 2000, and they also imply that mortality estimates are not correct for any individual. If we take a 65-year-old in 2000, the current life expectancy for that individual would be based on expected mortality rates for a 66-year-old in 2001, a 67-year-old in 2002, and so on. This will lead to underestimates of the cost of providing a pension.

Table 5 **Annual cost of £10,000 p.a. pension promise to a 60-year-old (based on GAD Period UK Mortality Table 2001–03)**

Age	Male pension	Female pension	Age	Male pension	Female pension
60	9,906	9,941			
61	9,799	9,875	81	4,718	6,221
62	9,684	9,803	82	4,312	5,855
63	9,558	9,726	83	3,914	5,472
64	9,422	9,644	84	3,515	5,074
65	9,276	9,552	85	3,127	4,662
66	9,119	9,453	86	2,722	4,226
67	8,949	9,345	87	2,344	3,790
68	8,762	9,227	88	1,990	3,354
69	8,561	9,097	89	1,662	2,929
70	8,340	8,955	90	1,360	2,514
71	8,107	8,801	91	1,101	2,123
72	7,850	8,630	92	877	1,761
73	7,576	8,439	93	679	1,430
74	7,280	8,230	94	513	1,129
75	6,962	8,004	95	382	876
76	6,625	7,754	96	275	661
77	6,271	7,487	97	194	487
78	5,901	7,200	98	132	349
79	5,521	6,895	99	89	243
80	5,122	6,569	100	58	166

cent) and 25 per cent of the 30-year rate (1.49 per cent) = 1.58 per cent.

Using 1.58 per cent as the discount rate, the NPV of pension Promise 3 is £167,346 for men and £190,894 for women (multiples of 16.7 and 19.1 respectively). Since we will use these values in our calculations below, I will call them the 'cost of Promise 3'.

What is promised?

We have calculated the cost of a simple promise (Promise 3) – but this is very different from the pension promises actually made to public sector workers. In what respects is this so?

As a result of years of bargaining, negotiation and compromise, the promises include not only a pension, but also many of the following:

- a pension for the surviving spouse, or (lately) civil partner;
- the ability to commute a portion of the pension to a tax-free lump sum, or in some cases a taxed sum;
- widow's or widower's pension and/or lump-sum benefit for death-in-service;
- early retirement in return for giving up some pension;
- an early retirement pension on health grounds;
- deferred pensions for those who leave employment;
- an option for employees to transfer out of the scheme in return for a cash sum now, or in return for benefits in another pension scheme.

Almost all these variations will add to the cost to the pension provider. The exceptions are the last two, and the last is the stark exception. Transfer values[18] in the past have under-priced the net present value of individual pensions, and have penalised transferees and benefited the employers.

In the methodology I will use to estimate public sector pension liabilities, and current pension costs, I will not need to analyse these elements in detail. I am going to concentrate on the

---

18 Except within the 'Public Sector Pension Club', where transfers can take place between these schemes without loss of value.

small number of key areas (discount rates; mortality; salary rises) which may account for significant under-reporting of the liabilities. This means that I will have to rely on the scheme actuary (usually GAD) to cover the other additional costs, noted above, adequately.

Final salary?

So far the calculations have been straightforward and more or less objective. There can be little dispute that the NPVs we have calculated in the 'Mortality' section are close to the index-linked annuity cost. We can check this with index-linked annuity providers for confirmation. Most do not provide exactly the same annuity as Promise 3, but multiples for the closest pension specification are about 23.9 for men and 25.1 for women[19] – much higher than our calculated 16.7 and 19.1. This reflects (a) their more conservative mortality assumptions (they include expected improvements in mortality and also buyers of annuities live longer than the UK average – people who are in poor health do not have a strong incentive to buy an annuity), (b) the interest rate risk they will have to take even with the best portfolio of matching index-linked gilts, and (c) the profit they need to make to cover their costs and their committed capital.

But none of this covers the much more complex liability that the final salary provider takes on – the linkage to final salary. This commitment means that the promise to most public sector workers who retire while working in the public sector (I will deal with those who don't in a minute) is more like this: 'Your

19 Sources: www.annuityadvisor.co.uk and www.prudential.co.uk.

employer promises to pay you a proportion of the best of the last (few) years' salary from your retirement date until you die. The proportion depends on your length of service, and the amount you receive when you retire will be index linked'. Let's call this 'Promise 4'.

This section will work out the variables that determine the starting pension amount – i.e. the £10,000 p.a. in all our previous examples. Once we have got the 'starting pension', we can easily calculate, from the analysis above, roughly how much the pension liability is.

Let's take some stylised rules of a pension scheme, to see if we can work out what pension is promised: accrual rate $\frac{1}{60}$[20]; retirement age 60; pension based on final year's salary.

Let us suppose, first, that the employee is in a lower-paid, lower-skilled job, in which there is no natural career progression. We will assume for this employee that his/her wages go up with average earnings, but no more. We will assume also that this employee works in the public sector scheme for his/her whole career (40 years – from age 20 to 60).

Average earnings rises have exceeded average price rises by around 2 per cent p.a. over the past 40 years. Figure 2 illustrates this.

This increase of 2 per cent p.a. is close to the real growth rate of the UK economy (and also labour productivity growth over this period), so it is logical to use 2 per cent as the 'assumed' earnings excess over RPI in this exercise. Let us also pick an assumed

---

20 $\frac{1}{60}$th is the rate for the post-2002 Civil Service 'Premium' pension scheme. Most other large schemes have $\frac{1}{80}$th, but they tend to give three-times-pension lump sums: the combination of the lump sum and the smaller pension is quite close to $\frac{1}{60}$th in value terms.

Figure 2   **UK earnings versus prices (index January 1963 = 100)**

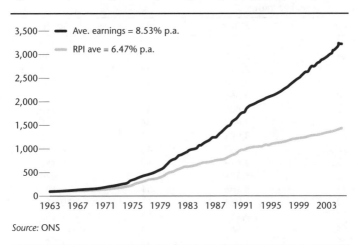

Ave. earnings = 8.53% p.a.

RPI ave = 6.47% p.a.

Source: ONS

inflation rate (for illustration purposes) of 3 per cent. Obviously over the past twenty or more years this has varied widely, but our assumption here is only for illustration purposes, because with index-linked gilts we will be able to eliminate this risk to the employer for the future.

Table 6 below shows the path of earnings for our fictional unskilled employee; I have assumed this employee's final salary to be £15,000 p.a., which they receive in their 59th year.

With 2 per cent real growth in the economy, and even with modest inflation, money wages rise enormously over 40 years.

This employee worked 40 completed years if he started work on his twentieth birthday, and this entitles him to a pension of $^{40}/_{60}$th of his final salary (£15,000), which is £10,000 p.a.

This provides us with all the information we need to answer the question: 'What proportion of salary, if paid as a constant

Table 6 **Salary progression for an unskilled worker (3% inflation; 2% real earnings; £)**

Age	Salary	Age	Salary
20	2,188	40	5,872
21	2,299	41	6,169
22	2,415	42	6,481
23	2,537	43	6,809
24	2,666	44	7,154
25	2,800	45	7,516
26	2,942	46	7,896
27	3,091	47	8,295
28	3,247	48	8,715
29	3,412	49	9,156
30	3,584	50	9,620
31	3,766	51	10,106
32	3,956	52	10,618
33	4,156	53	11,155
34	4,367	54	11,719
35	4,588	55	12,312
36	4,820	56	12,935
37	5,064	57	13,590
38	5,320	58	14,278
39	5,589	59	15,000

percentage, will be needed to pay for this pension?' Let us start with males. We know from the 'Mortality' section above that the cost of Promise 3 (i.e. a pension of £10,000 p.a. index linked) is £167,346. So the simple question is: 'What fixed proportion of the annual salaries in Table 6 needs to be invested each year to make £167,346 on the day the employee retires?' Remember that to take no inflation or investment risk, the employer will invest in the same instruments as for the annuity – namely index-linked gilts. For this average twenty-year investment (ranging from one to 40 years), we will use the nineteen-year real interest rate (1.61 per cent from June 2005 data). Unfortunately for the employer, there is no investment that matches earnings.[21]

This sets us up for the first calculation. Table 7 shows this calculation.

The 'investment pot' is calculated as [the prior-year 'investment pot' $\times$ (1 + inflation) $\times$ (1+ real return)] + the current year's contribution.[22] Excel 'Goal Seek' is used to find the contribution rate that gave £167,346 at the end of the 59th year. That contribution rate is 30%. Note that this calculation finds the average contribution rate over the 40-year period. We can undertake a more detailed approach to the same problem which can find the contribution rate for each year that will be sufficient to pay for the cost of pension accrued in a specific year; this rises with age and length in the scheme. I will not pursue this point further.

We can do the same for females: the calculation is exactly the same as in Table 7, but with the higher amount needed at maturity (£190,894 rather than £167,346). The result is an annual average contribution of 34.25 per cent of salary for 40 years.

So what these calculations are telling us is that either the employee or the employer or both must set aside 30 per cent of

---

21 If there were, for example, a gilt that provided guaranteed returns relative to average earnings then, on current interest rates, the market would price the yield to be just negative (expected excess of earnings over prices of *c*. 2 per cent; current real yield 1.5 per cent). So unless the employer chooses to take much more investment risk by investing in equities (which in the long run tend to give returns arguably more in line with GDP – and therefore earnings – growth), then he has to take earnings risk – risk that is related not to average earnings in the economy, but to earnings in their specific sector.

22 I do not make an allowance here (nor in any of the calculations) for that small proportion of employees who die in service, and thereby cross-subsidise their surviving co-workers. This is because most of the public sector schemes have generous widow's pensions/death-in-service benefits, which reduce this subsidy to negligible proportions.

Table 7 Annual contribution to provide a male ²/₃ final salary pension (£)

Final salary £	15,000	10,000
Inflation rate p.a.	3.00%	Pension: Amount needed (male) 167,346
Average earnings excess over inflation p.a.	2.00%	Contribution rate 30.02%
Real return p.a.	1.61%	

Age	Salary	Contribution	'Investment pot'	Age	Salary	Contribution	'Investment pot'
20	2,188	786	657	40	5,872	2,109	35,642
21	2,299	825	1,378	41	6,169	2,215	39,155
22	2,415	867	2,167	42	6,481	2,327	42,924
23	2,537	911	3,030	43	6,809	2,445	46,968
24	2,666	957	3,971	44	7,154	2,569	51,304
25	2,800	1,006	4,997	45	7,516	2,699	55,951
26	2,942	1,056	6,113	46	7,896	2,835	60,928
27	3,091	1,110	7,326	47	8,295	2,979	66,257
28	3,247	1,166	8,642	48	8,715	3,130	71,960
29	3,412	1,225	10,069	49	9,156	3,288	78,061
30	3,584	1,287	11,614	50	9,620	3,454	84,586
31	3,766	1,352	13,286	51	10,106	3,629	91,560
32	3,956	1,421	15,093	52	10,618	3,813	99,014
33	4,156	1,493	17,044	53	11,155	4,006	106,975
34	4,367	1,568	19,149	54	11,719	4,208	115,477
35	4,588	1,647	21,418	55	12,312	4,421	124,553
36	4,820	1,731	23,863	56	12,935	4,645	134,239
37	5,064	1,818	26,495	57	13,590	4,880	144,573
38	5,320	1,910	29,327	58	14,278	5,127	155,594
39	5,589	2,007	32,371	59	15,000	5,386	167,346

annual salary for a male, and 34 per cent for a female, each year for 40 years to achieve sufficient money in the 'investment pot' to cover the cost of a $^2/_3$ index-linked final salary pension for an employee who experiences no career progression.

Investment in equities and other higher-yielding investments only reduces the cost of meeting the pension promise at the expense of higher risk (see Box 1 on page 53). Table 7 represents the best answer to the question 'how much does a pension cost?' It does not attempt to answer the question 'but what can I do to lower the cost, and at what risk?' That is a separate question, one that all funded final salary pension schemes have to address.

In the case of unfunded government occupational pension schemes, however, not only is the second question irrelevant because there is no funding, but conveniently for this calculation the cost to the government from deferring index-linked expenditure now to some point in the future (and the return to the government from bringing such expenditure forward) is exactly the current index-linked gilt yield – since the government can both borrow and lend (by repaying borrowing) at exactly the current market rate. This point is crucial. The government has a choice. It could offer employees higher pay now in return for lower pension promises (which might be popular with, and acceptable to, their employees). It can borrow money at the rate of return on index-linked gilts in order to finance the payment of higher wages now, and will effectively repay the borrowing by avoiding the future payment that the pension promise would have incurred had it remained unchanged. It is therefore possible to imagine a trade-off that would be both attractive to employees and cheaper for the government.[23]

Career progression

The story is about to get worse from the employer's point of view, because most government employees are not on fixed pay levels. Most grades have escalating pay scales, and many employees will achieve promotion to higher grades during their careers. Few (if any) will be demoted to lower grades later in life, and fewer, if any, will go down the pay scales within grades. Of course, people will come and go, and I will look at that at the end of this section.

We can recalculate the figures in Table 7, but this time we can build in career progression. As an example of strong career progression (to illustrate the point), I will assume that a successful professional in the pubic service might expect to progress with salary increases of 3 per cent p.a. above the rate of average earnings. This will give a 'real' increase (over average earnings) of about 3.2 times over a 40-year career. This means a young graduate who starts on £22,000 today would end his career earning £71,000 in today's money. This seems reasonable for a professional career.

---

23   Assume that the rate of return on index-linked gilts is 1.5 per cent.The government can bring forward the cash costs of employment by raising salaries, lowering pension promises and borrowing to finance higher current salaries at 1.5 per cent real. The government will eventually have to repay the borrowing plus interest at 1.5 cent real per year, of course, but this will simply be instead of the pensions that it would have had to pay if it had not reduced the pension promises.

Box 1 **The cost of a pension**

In my opinion the issue of the 'cost of a pension' has attracted an extraordinarily high level of debate for a question that has a definitive answer. Let me use this analogy.

I am an employer, and I pay an employee £15,000 per year. The employee receives £1,250 monthly in arrears. I would expect no debate on the question 'how much does that employee cost to employ?'

Now suppose that the employer has identified a particularly astute professional punter. This man has a good record of making more money on the horses than he loses, and, for a small fee, gives the employer his tips. The employer makes a practice of making bets at the start of each month with the £1,250 set aside for his employee's wages that month. Sometimes it is a disaster and all the month's wages are lost. Other months are terrific, and the employer makes several times the monthly salary as profit. The employer, of course, makes up or receives the difference whatever the outcome, so that the employee never really knows what the employer is doing, and is perfectly content with his pay arrangements. Let us imagine that, over the years, the employer makes an average of 33 per cent profit on each monthly bet (after the fee to the punter), so the average annual cost to the employer is £10,000. What is the cost of employment?

I would wish the reader to agree that the cost of employment should universally be taken to be £15,000 p.a., with an offsetting credit (in this case of £5,000 p.a.) for successful betting (and reported as such). Indeed, in these circumstances I would question whether the employer would not be better off closing his business and spending more of his time at the races!

This debate has boiled down to the appropriate discount rate for pension liabilities. I am using around 1.6 per cent real, because that is the current market price, and is available now to every investor in the UK who wishes to acquire an index-linked investment at no risk. Those who wish to have the employee's cost at £10,000 will wish to use higher rates of return (which may reduce the 'apparent' cost of the pension), but which are not available without risk.

It is entirely logical for the sponsor of a funded defined-benefit pension fund to choose to accept some investment risk in return for the expectation of higher returns for the pension fund over the longer term. It is a business decision, and employers make and remake these kinds of decisions all the time. What is not acceptable, however, is to use this choice as a lever to argue that because of this the liabilities of the fund are somehow reduced. The liabilities are invariant with respect to the method of investment: they exist because of pension promises, and will have to be paid whatever the investment returns.[24]

Actuaries in the UK until recently used a 9 per cent discount rate for active members; they now tend to use the nominal bond rate for AA-rated companies. This is now the rate required by FRS17, which is the accountants' standard for company

---

24 There are some (including the UK Accounting Standards Board) who argue (implicitly) that pension promises are subject to default in the case of sponsor bankruptcy, and therefore pension liabilities deserve a higher discount rate than risk free. To accept this is to accept the failure of the pension funding system – whose entire *raison d'être* is to protect against this eventuality. The government's regulatory weakness in this area is deplorable, and I argue strongly for a proper restoration of full funding at buy-out/risk-free liabilities. Whatever the merits of this argument, none of it applies to government pension liabilities, where non-payment through sponsor bankruptcy is not an option.

accounts. The government currently uses 3.5 per cent real, although it is planned that this will go down – to 2.8 per cent – in the financial year 2005/06.[25]

Just how sensitive the cost of pensions is to changes in the real interest rate we can see if we use 3.5 per cent p.a. instead of 1.6 per cent p.a. for Table 7 (and the annuity cost). We get annual contribution rates of 17 per cent (males) and 19 per cent (females). Compare these with 30 per cent (males) and 34 per cent (females) with exactly the same calculation, but at current market interest rates. This sensitivity is illustrated in Figure 8 in the next chapter.

---

25 These values are approved by the government-sponsored Financial Reporting Advisory Board. Quoting from the seventh report (my italics!):

'… Section 2.10. … the Board noted that it had accepted that the discount rate for pension scheme liabilities promulgated by the Treasury on the advice of the Government Actuary's Department should remain at 3.5 per cent in real terms for accounting periods prior to 2005–06. *This rate was based on a review of long-term historical patterns of real rates of return on gilts.* However, as also noted in the Board's sixth report, the Treasury accepted the Board's proposal that the discount rate ought to be set in line with the requirements of the FRS: the AA corporate bond rate. The Board agreed that, in order to achieve budgetary certainty, the rate would be reviewed for each Spending Review period.

Section 2.11 The Treasury reported to the Board at its March 2004 meeting that the Government Actuary's Department had concluded its review of the discount rate for provisions for pension scheme liabilities. Based on the yields of AA corporate bonds with maturity dates of more than 15 years, measured over a three month period, the Actuary has determined that the rate to be used, with effect from 2005–06, in discounting pension provisions is 2.8 per cent real. The impact of a reduction in the discount rate is an increase in the level of the provisions; the overall impact of the change will be accounted for in Central Government Accounts for 2005–06 …'

If we build this progression into Table 7, we can calculate annual contribution rates of 49 per cent for males, and 56 per cent for females. These are very high contribution rates, and a different order of magnitude from those commonly believed to be sufficient to cover the accrual of liability for a ⅔ final salary pension scheme. Real high-flyers (say on a 5 per cent p.a. increase in salaries over earnings – that is someone who starts on a salary of £22,000 and ends on a salary of £147,000 in today's money) require contribution rates of 64 per cent for males and 73 per cent for females.

Early leavers

All is not gloom and doom for employers, and in one area they have provided themselves with an attractive break – this is the area of early leavers.

There are two ways in which an employer penalises the employee upon departure from the pension scheme. The first is by the way that a pre-retirement leaver's deferred pension is calculated.

In most pubic sector schemes, the leaver's final salary is used as the base for the year's entitlement calculation, and that final salary is uprated each year by the RPI.[26] While this might seem perfectly reasonable, it denies the departing employee any benefit from increases not only in general earnings levels, but also in his own salary. This is entirely understandable on the part of the employer, but it is costly to the employee.

---

26 Until comparatively recently, there was no RPI uprating for deferred pensioners at all in many schemes. This was particularly penal in periods of high inflation. Even today, private sector schemes do not fully uprate deferred pensions in line with inflation.

As an example, on the assumptions I have made to date, assume an employee leaves public sector employment on his 40th birthday after twenty years' work. While all this is calculable only with the benefit of hindsight, we would find that the employer is required to contribute only 21 per cent of his salary for twenty years, rather than 30 per cent of salary had the employee stayed in the scheme for his whole career (calculated in Table 7). Looked at in terms of the 'investment pot' required, the employee makes a 'gift' to the employer (in this case) of £9,719 on his departure date, which is the difference in the 'investment pot' needed for continuing employment (£32,371 at aged 39 in Table 7) and £22,652 for the early leaver. This is 1½ years' salary at age 40 'given up'.

We can do exactly the same calculation for females, and we find that the *ex post* required contribution rate falls from 34 per cent of annual salary for continuous employment to 24 per cent p.a. when the employee works for only twenty years and has the pension deferred for twenty years.

Cash alternatives

Almost all defined-benefit pension funds, public and private, offer the opportunity for members to leave, and take a cash lump sum, supposedly equivalent to the value of their embedded pension. The idea is that this pot can be invested in another pension scheme to provide equivalent benefits.

The practice has been very different. Until relatively recently, cash payments for pension leavers were set way below their economic value, or perhaps more accurately were calculated using patently unrealistic assumptions. While there is now legislation and standardised practice[27] which has tightened up the worst abuses, nevertheless it remains the case that early leavers who opt for cash in lieu of deferred pension will cross-subsidise continuing employees. The corollary, therefore, is that this is a source of relief for the hard-pressed employer.[28]

Summary

This chapter has run through the various levels of calculation needed to make an informed estimate of the costs of providing a final salary index-linked pension. I have made no attempt to model fully any actual scheme: that is the topic of the next chapter.

---

27 For example, the Institute of Actuaries GN11 Practice Standard.
28 It is worth mentioning that this can be balanced by transfers into the schemes by new public sector employees who bring with them a transfer value from a previous scheme. This is likely to be rare in most public sector employment.

3 ESTIMATING CURRENT PUBLIC SECTOR PENSION SCHEME LIABILITIES AND RUNNING COST

Unrealistic assumptions

As explained earlier in this paper, the approach I am going to take in this section is to use the maths we have developed in Chapter 2 to calculate estimates of the effect of varying assumptions embedded within official estimates of public pension liabilities. But which assumptions should we vary? Any estimate of an employer's pension liability requires a very large number of assumptions; many are employee specific, many scheme specific, and many exert only a minor influence on liability valuations.

So my methodology will be as follows:

- gather the latest official valuations of unfunded public sector liabilities;
- gather key scheme assumptions;
- find official estimates of sensitivity of the liabilities to these assumptions (if any);
- develop our own sensitivity estimates for both variables from first principles (using the Chapter 2 methodology);
- choose realistic assumptions;
- use these values to calculate our own estimates of public sector pension liabilities.

I will then go on to calculate an estimate of the annual cost to the average public sector employer of providing a pension – i.e. the economic cost, not the 'cash' cost – expressed as a percentage of pay. It is this value which is really important, since it can be the legitimate subject of policy decisions, whereas existing liabilities are largely immutable without expropriating existing rights from members.

Finally, I will use official information on changes in liabilities over time to attempt to reconcile my estimates of 'economic cost' and official estimates of 'cash' costs and increases in liabilities.

Liabilities

I have collected the unfunded public sector liabilities valuations reported by GAD over the years (mainly via parliamentary written answers). To my knowledge there is a two-year gap in reporting. Interpolating the years for which no consolidated data was published, however, we can build up eight years of data:

Table 8 **Total public sector unfunded occupational pension liabilities**

Year end	£ billion
March 1998	295
March 1999	310[1]
March 2000	330
March 2001	350
March 2002	380
March 2003	425
March 2004	460
March 2005	530

Source: Government Actuary's Department (various written parliamentary answers)

1   Data not available for 1999 and 2000 – author's estimates.

The objective is to reach an estimate for liabilities as at 31 March 2006, adjusted to take account of more reasonable assumptions, and as a base we need to make an assessment of the likely liabilities that GAD will report for this date.

At the time of writing, all the main public sector pension schemes have published their 2004/05 resource accounts,[2] and these have given us a very good picture of how their liabilities change in response to the changing interest rates at which they are valued – because the four main schemes announced that they will have moved from a 3.5 per cent p.a. assumed real discount rate on 31 March 2005 to a 2.8 per cent p.a. assumed real discount from 1 April 2005. We will call this concept the 'elasticity' of their liability with respect to changing interest rates. Table 9 shows this information for the four main schemes, together with a calculation of the implied real interest rate elasticity of the liabilities.

Since we know that the interest rate used by these schemes went down from 3.5 per cent to 2.8 per cent on 1 April 2005, we will be able to use this information on the elasticity of the value of the liabilities to changes in interest rates to estimate the government's own estimate of liabilities for March 2006. We also need to estimate the other components of the change in the liability.

2   While all public sector resource accounts have by law to be laid before Parliament by 31 January in the year following that to which they relate (i.e. 31 January 2006 for the 2004/05 accounts), the NHS Pensions Resource Accounts 2004/05 (House of Commons Paper 764), which were 'approved' by Parliament on 30 January 2006, were not published until 12 April 2006, and before that date were nowhere to be found – even by MPs who had approved them! Even by May 2006 the NHS Pensions Accounts 2004/05 were still not available on the NHS pensions website. This document alone accounts for a rise in pension liabilities in the year to March 2005 of £23.5 billion – so it strikes me as odd that such an important document is not readily available to the public over thirteen months after the end of the period to which it relates.

Table 9 **Official estimates of liabilities' interest rate elasticity at March 2005**

	31 March 2005 liability	*1 April 2005 liability*	*Percentage change*	*Duration[3] over this range*
NHS	£127.9 billion	£145.8 billion	14.0	20.0
Teachers	£119.7 billion	£131.5 billion	9.9	14.1
Civil Service	£84.1 billion	£94.7 billion	12.6	18.0
Armed forces	£66.5 billion	£76.5 billion	15.0	21.5
Total	**£398.2 billion**	**£448.5 billion**	**12.6**	**18.0**

Source: 2004/05 scheme resource accounts

In Table 15 in Appendix 3, I show a forecast of the various elements of the annual change of the pension liabilities between March 2005 and March 2006, including the one-off change on 1 April 2005 arising from the change in the official discount rate. I use PESA[4] and GAD official figures, and my forecast is of the size of the annual adjustment (error term), which relates to inaccurate actuarial assumptions in the schemes.

In coming to an estimate of the annual error term, I have calculated the error terms from the last few years' reconciliations of out-turn liabilities figures. Table 10 shows this progression in the past five years (the detail for 2003/04 and 2004/05 is shown in Tables 13 and 14 respectively in Appendix 2).

The year ending March 2005 was unusual for two reasons – there was an overdue actuarial valuation in the largest scheme (the NHS), and the police and fire schemes had their discount rates lowered (to 2.4 per cent p.a.). I estimate that for the year ending March 2006 the error term will be much smaller – and I am estimating £15 billion. I still believe that there are some

---

3　See below for a definition of duration. Calculation for, e.g., the NHS is 14.0%/ (3.5%–2.8%) = 20.

4　Public Expenditure Statistical Analysis (PESA), 2005, Table B.1.

Table 10 **Error terms derived from reconciling PESA 2005 with GAD liabilities out-turns**

Year ending March	2001	2002	2003	2004	2005
Error term (£ billion)	7.8	8.6	26.8	13.4	40.0

optimistic assumptions embedded within the current scheme assumptions, and this forecast is consistent with this view.

This gives us my forecast of the government's figures for the March 2006 public sector pension liabilities of £639 billion (note: this is my estimate of the liability the government will announce – not my estimate of liability). This figure will be announced at the end of 2006 or the beginning of 2007 if recent practice is followed.

With this information, we can now show the progression of liabilities as a graph to March 2006 (Figure 3).

The first question to ask is 'why are the liabilities rising so rapidly, when the public sector pension schemes are reason-

Figure 3   **Public sector unfunded pension liabilities**

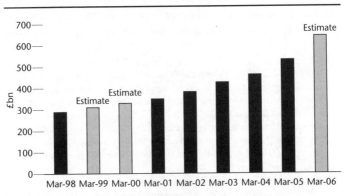

Source: Government Actuary's Department; author's estimates

ably mature?' This is particularly odd when, according to the government, new pensions liabilities taken on each year were lower than the pensions paid each year until 2003/04.[5] At first glance, one would imagine that this should have meant that total liabilities were going *down*. Remember, however, that the government has not set aside any money to pay these pensions. Therefore each year there is a large interest charge, raising the liabilities as the discount rate unwinds (see Chapter 2 for the theory and PESA 2005 for the numbers), without any investment returns from assets to compensate. One can think of pensions paid each year as including an element of rolled-up interest repayment, and therefore, unless the pensions in payment are larger than the sum of new liabilities from service and the interest charge (which will include inflation), then the liabilities will keep rising.[6] Second, there is clearly a large gap between the assumptions under which the valuation of liabilities is made and the actual experience in the public sector pension funds in recent years. This is reflected in the figures in Table 10.

Once all the systematic errors have been corrected,[7] one can think of pension funds' liabilities as being a very long-lagged moving average of past earnings growth, which will in the very longest term

---

5   Source: ibid. Compare the top line ('Change in liability' – basically the current cost of the year's additional service for members) and the penultimate line ('Pensions in payment'). For 2003/04 and prior years 'Pensions in payment' were *higher* than 'Change in liability'.

6   For example, say the interest rate was 10 per cent and there was a liability to pay out £100 on 1 January 2007. On 31 December 2006 the liability would be 100/1.1 = 90.9. On 31 December 2006 the liability is 100 because it is just about to be paid. The liabilities become bigger as fulfilment of the promised payments approaches.

7   I say 'systematic' because all assumptions about future behaviour and economics are just that. Good forecasting requires assumptions which are equally frequently found to be too pessimistic as too optimistic. Systematically biased assumptions are always or almost always found to be wrong in the same direction.

keep pace with earnings, and therefore exceed RPI growth. So even if we account in 'real' terms (i.e. adjusted for price inflation), it will still appear that pension liabilities keep on growing.

Estimate of liabilities

Let us turn now to attempting a realistic (i.e. neither optimistic nor pessimistic) estimate of public sector occupational pension liabilities at end-March 2006. I see my task as being to strip out optimism in the assumptions that GAD makes for the main public sector schemes without introducing any elements of undue pessimism.

From the 'first principles' exercise in Chapter 2, we know that there are three overriding assumptions that dominate the liabilities calculation – salary growth; longevity; and the appropriate discount rate.

Salary growth assumptions
In the case of salary growth, GAD has assumed 1.5 per cent real growth in future salaries across the board (before accounting separately for career-progression-related increases). With the benefit of hindsight, this has proved to be too low for the years 2000–05, when salary growth in the public sector has been exceptionally high. Over that period, average real earnings have grown at 2.23 per cent p.a. for the public sector as a whole, and at 3.12 per cent p.a. for the health sub-index.[8] In adjusting this

---

8   Sources: ONS – Average Earnings Index – Public Sector (LNNJ); and Average Earnings Supplementary Tables Public Sector Series – Health series. I calculate compound rates of growth over the five years to August 2005 (4.69 per cent p.a. and 5.59 per cent p.a. respectively) and subtract the compound growth of the RPI index over the same period (2.47 per cent).

assumption in my calculations, I will use 2 per cent p.a. future increases over RPI, not 1.5 per cent p.a. This is lower than recent history, but is broadly in line with long-term economy-wide real earnings growth. The effect of this amendment is to change the liabilities of all the active members (i.e. those working in the public sector), but not those in respect of pensioners or scheme members with deferred pensions – the liabilities to these groups are not linked to salaries, only to RPI.[9]

Active members account for 60 per cent[10] of the net present value of the public sector schemes (discounted at a rate of interest of 1.12 per cent real). The effect of raising the salary growth assumption from 1.5 per cent to 2.0 per cent for active members can be calculated using the principles in Table 7. It transpires that this increases the contribution rate required (and hence the scale of the liabilities) by 9.9 per cent, and so will increase overall liabilities by 60 per cent × 9.9 per cent = 5.9 per cent. This is the value I will use to adjust liabilities for our differing salary assumptions.

Mortality assumptions

We have seen from data earlier in this paper that longevity has been on a long-term upward trend. Mortality assumptions in all the public sector schemes are determined at the time of the

9   In passing it is worth making the point that when pay increases in the public sector at a particularly high rate, for one reason or another, the whole stock of pension liabilities for active members, accumulated to date, including those liabilities for past years' service, increases in line with the increase in pay.

10   Source: HM Treasury press release, March 2006, which puts the active weight at 50 per cent discounted at 3.5 per cent p.a. I have adjusted this value upwards by 20 per cent (i.e. to 60 per cent) to take account of the artificially high discount rate the schemes are using – this affects active member liabilities more than other scheme liabilites.

actuarial reviews, which occur at frequencies between three and five years. There are a lot of vignettes in the actuarial reviews which make it clear that many of the actuarial assumptions are being found to be over-optimistic.[11]

There are two effects of long gaps between reviews combined with improvements in mortality. The first is that there are 'each-year' adjustments in between (i.e. line 7 in Tables 13 and 14); and the second is that at the time of each review there is likely to be a significant upward shift in liabilities as the 'each-year' adjustments are planned to be eliminated at the review by changes in assumptions (to allow for lower mortality), and the present value of the changes to the liabilities caused by the adjustment is calculated.[12]

Clearly increased longevity is capable of exerting a very substantial influence on overall liabilities, since an extra year's average life from 79 to 80 is not an addition of $\frac{1}{80}$th to the liabilities, but more like $\frac{1}{20}$th[13] (since retirement is at 60). Just taking the crudest observation, longevity in the UK has increased by 0.21 years (for men) and 0.18 years (for women) for every year that has passed in the past twenty (see Figure 1); this will tend to increase pension liabilities (very roughly and other things being equal) by about 0.9 per cent p.a. for men, and by 0.65 per cent p.a. for women. In the context of the end-2003 liability of £425 billion, this is about £3.4 billion p.a.

---

11 E.g.: '… mortality experience of the existing cohort of ill-health pensioners has been unexpectedly light …'; '… For widows … mortality experience was lighter than the assumptions adopted for the previous review …'; March 2001 Teachers' Review (published March 2003).

12 That is, the present value of the stream of future 'error charges' is taken into the liabilities' valuation; and thereafter the annual 'error charge' is eliminated.

13 But not exactly because of the effect of discounting.

We know from Table 10 that public sector schemes have a consistent record of underestimating future liabilities through over-optimism in their assumptions. We are looking in the mortality context for a one-off adjustment which will mean that future error terms are evenly distributed around zero. That, in my opinion, means a revision in longevity improvement assumptions.

My estimate is that we are more likely to avoid having to alter mortality assumptions in the future if we assume liabilities that are, say, 0.5 per cent per year higher than existing assumptions (lower than 1 per cent to account for a slowing of the improving mortality trend and the existing trend assumptions). This is relatively easy to model: it is like reducing the real discount rate on liabilities by 0.5 per cent p.a. The effect this has on public sector pension liabilities (valued at market real interest rates) is to increase liabilities by 10.2 per cent.[14] In the year ending March 2005, however, the NHS pension scheme substantially revised its actuarial assumptions, creating a one-off increase in the liabilities of £14.9 billion,[15] or 14.3 per cent of the March 2004 liabilities. I consider that this one-off change has largely eliminated optimism on mortality in the NHS scheme (which accounts for a quarter of the total public sector liability), so I will reduce my estimate of the mortality adjustment downwards to 75 per cent of 10.2 per cent, i.e. 7.6 per cent. This is the figure I will use to adjust liabilities on the basis of over-optimistic mortality assumptions.

14   See the 'Real interest rate assumption' section below for details of the effect of changing discount rates on liabilities.

15   Source: NHS Pension Scheme Resource Accounts, 2004/05, p. 20, para. 5.

This figure of 7.6 per cent compares with a lower adjustment, 3 per cent, that Watson Wyatt[16] make to adjust for the government's over-optimistic mortality assumptions.

Real interest rate assumption

From the previous chapter it will already be clear that I believe that public sector pension liabilities should be discounted at the market real interest rate. By far the best market for this is index-linked gilts; particularly so because (as we have already seen) the schemes themselves run 'notional' funds comprising solely index-linked gilts to 'notionally fund' their liabilities. Also, the employers have a choice of offering pensions in the future or increasing pay now to compensate for the loss of pension. If the employers were to increase pay now, the government could borrow to finance this at the real rate of return on index-linked gilts. The real yield on index-linked gilts is variable, and therefore time-specific to March 2006 for all that follows; but there is a definitive value as long as we know the duration of the liability – and therefore the maturity of the index-linked gilt we need to look at. We need to calculate the average duration[17] of these liabilities – information we also require to assess the sensitivity of the value of the liabilities to

16   In their 17 February 2005 press release, Watson Wyatt chose to increase the GAD-reported liabilities by 5 per cent to account for GAD's over-optimistic mortality assumptions, although they gave no reasoning or data in their press release to support this estimate. In their 8 March 2006 press release, they chose to increase liabilities by 3 per cent.

17   'Duration' is a measure of the average maturity of a series of cash flows. A convenient feature of duration is that the duration in years roughly corresponds to the elasticity of the present value of the cash flows with respect to interest rates. So a liability with a duration of twenty years will experience a change in value of the net present value of 20 per cent for every 1 per cent movement in interest rates.

changes in real interest rates. By chance (i.e. because there was a discount rate change on 1 April 2005), we have good information on average duration, and this has already been shown in Table 9. So we have an average duration in the real interest rate range 3.5 per cent to 2.8 per cent of eighteen years.

Just for reference, the real yield at this duration is 1.12 per cent p.a. on 31 March 2006.

We can, however, be rather more sophisticated than this. Really accurate discounting of future cash flows (which is what pension liabilities are) requires interest rates appropriate for the time at which each individual cash flow is received – to be completely accurate, each cash flow should be discounted separately at the real interest rate appropriate to the time at which the cash flow is to be received. The index-linked gilt market can give us this information. We can also calculate the shape of the cash flows embedded within the public sector pension liabilities by building a model of the future cash flows using the liabilities' elasticity revealed by the reduction in the across-the-board discount rate from 3.5 per cent p.a. to 2.8 per cent p.a. With this information, we can apply the 31 March 2006 real interest rate curve derived from the index-linked gilt market to the model cash flows. This will give us the most accurate estimate of the effect of the (lower) market interest rates, particularly in view of the (quite steep) downward-sloping real yield curve on this date. Figure 4 shows the index-linked market yield curve at 31 March 2006, interpolated for missing maturity years. Note that the government issued its first ultra-long (50-year) index-linked gilt in September 2005, and this allows us accurate pricing at these long (but highly relevant) horizons.

Figure 4   **Real yield curve, 31 March 2006**

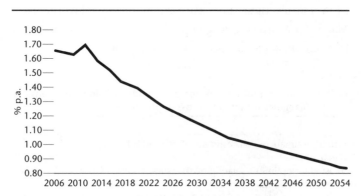

Source: Debt Management Office I/L Gilts Prices; linear interpolation

To complete a valuation of pension liabilities, we need an interest rate to use at horizons longer than 50 years. For this purpose I plan to assume that the curve stops its downward slope, and continues flat at 0.83 per cent out to the date of the last liability that the model calculates – about 2086.

It turns out that using the above yield curve increases the liabilities that have been calculated on the basis of 2.8 per cent p.a. by 40.8 per cent.[18]

---

18   This is more accurate than the 'back of the envelope' calculation, which is (2.8 per cent–1.1 per cent) = 1.7 per cent x 18 (duration) = 30.6 per cent rise, because of two effects. The dominant effect is a phenomenon known as convexity, which (in this context) is the tendency of the duration of fixed cash flows to rise as the interest rate goes down. The second effect is the higher sensitivity of longer horizon cash flows to lower interest rates (and the curve is strongly downward sloping), which means that using one interest rate rather than discounting cash flows at varying appropriate interest rates modestly understates the change.

Summary

I can now use these three key assumptions to adjust the likely March 2006 GAD estimate of public sector pension liabilities to take account of the changed assumptions above.

Table 11 **Adjusting total public sector unfunded occupational pension liabilities for unrealistic assumptions**

	£ billion
Author's estimate of GAD estimate of pension liabilities, March 2005	639[19]
Adjusted for optimistic salary growth assumption (+ 5.9 per cent)	677
Adjusted for optimistic mortality assumption (+ 7.6 per cent)	728
Adjusted for unrealistic real interest rate assumption (+ 40.8 per cent)	**1,025**

This value for the total public sector pension liabilities at 31 March 2006 of £1,025 billion is higher than any previous number reported, even by independent observers, although Watson Wyatt used very similar methodology to produce the closest published figure of £960 billion.[20]

To put it in context, £1,025 billion compares with the £470 billion as the market value of all outstanding UK gilts[21] at 31 March 2006, and £456 billion for the government's calculation of public

---

19 Should GAD's estimate turn out to be higher (or lower), then the author's estimates for the adjusted figure would be correspondingly higher (or lower).

20 Watson Wyatt press release, 8 March 2006.

21 Source: DMO quarterly reviews to December 2005, plus author's estimates for Q1 2006.

sector net debt[22] on the same date. It represents 83 per cent of GDP, and if we account 'interest' on this debt as the sum of inflation and the real interest rate,[23] the government's annual interest bill on this £1,025 billion is £35.9 billion, or 2.9 per cent of GDP.

Headline outstanding liability

I think that very large numbers like this do not by themselves resonate with the public at large – they are too big to contemplate effectively. A couple of things are worth saying, however.

1 This liability is a debt – a government debt just like gilts.
2 This debt will incur interest until it is repaid.[24]

---

22 This definition differs from the Maastricht criteria of government indebtedness (which is calculated gross, and so produces a higher number). Public sector net debt is composed of outstanding gilts at nominal prices (some £50 billion lower than at market prices in March 2006), plus Treasury bills and short-term borrowing, plus National Savings obligations (about £68 billion in March 2006), plus other sterling and foreign currency debt, less financial assets (principally sterling cash balances plus the (substantial – about £27 billion) foreign currency reserves). Sources: DMO; National Savings; ONS; Bank of England; HM Treasury (mainly 2005 pre-Budget report); author's estimates for latest quarter.

23 Based on March 2006 year-on-year RPI inflation of 2.4 per cent p.a; and real interest of 1.1 per cent p.a. (the eighteen-year duration point on the 31 March 2006 real yield curve) = total interest 3.5 per cent p.a.

24 In so far as pensions are deferred pay, one could regard the pension promise given to an employee as an alternative to a pay increase (see also the discussion later). For a given level of taxes, the government would have to borrow more to provide the employee with immediate rather than deferred pay. In a very real sense, the pension promise (a promise to workers of future pay in the form of pension rather than pay today) is a form of government borrowing and, if the government really intends to meet its pension promises, this debt should be valued at a real interest rate equal to the real interest rate on index-linked bonds.

The repayment of this debt is going to occur over a very long period. The payment of interest on pension debt is rolled up and is finally repaid in the form of pensions. A pension promise is like a deep-discount security – it increases in value every year as the repayment date approaches (when interest is paid at maturity along with the principal), but no interest changes hands in the interim. Just because the interest is not paid in cash, however, policy-makers and employers need to be aware that the interest cost is a drain on the Exchequer just like any other item of public expenditure. This drain will be apparent as ever-increasing levels of pension liabilities materialise.

If this concept is difficult to grasp, we should remind ourselves that £1,025 billion is not the amount of the debt that the government has to repay. The amount that the government will have to repay is the undiscounted value of all the pension liabilities. We can estimate this value by replacing a 1.1 per cent real interest rate with 0 per cent real in our model (thus simply adding up the total of future real cash flows in the form of pensions already promised) and uprating all the future payments by an appropriate estimate of future inflation. The most appropriate estimate of future inflation can be found by examining the yields on index-linked gilts and those on conventional gilts. Because the latter do not compensate the investor for inflation and the former do, the difference between the yields is a good estimate of RPI expectations. A slightly more sophisticated version of this relationship is known as 'implied inflation', and this value was 2.95 per cent[25] per annum for the 2035 index-linked gilt at 31 December 2005. Using all the information derived in this study about the maturity structure of

---

25   Source: DMO quarterly review, December 2005.

the pension liabilities, I estimate the total nominal amount that the government can expect to have to pay over the next 80-odd years on current liabilities (i.e. not including any future service from public sector employees) to be £3,762 billion. Even if we exclude inflation (i.e. price the liability at today's prices), the raw liability is £1,406 billion (114 per cent of GDP).

A glimpse into the future

The value I have ascribed to the Government's pensions liabilities, and the official valuations, will tend to converge with the passage of time. If the Government continues to use a real discount rate higher than the market rate (2.8 per cent for 2005/6 accounts onwards), then the 'interest' payable on its calculated pension debt will be 2.8 per cent plus the rate of inflation. This interest will roll up in the official valuation, pushing it ever higher (and towards my valuation) as time goes on. My valuation will only accrue interest at 1.1 per cent plus inflation – the average market rate for index-linked debt. The picture is complicated by the relative maturity of each scheme – immature schemes will still generate future net liabilities, but may have more contributions than pensions payable, whereas schemes in equilibrium should pay out in pensions roughly the same as contributions (or actually a lot more in this case, since the contribution rate is too low), and mature pension schemes (e.g. those with a declining workforce) will see more pensions paid out than contributions, and a declining liability. The future path of each scheme's sector salary growth will also have an important influence. To put it another way, if my estimates of future liabilities are more accurate, the government will eventually have to pay out the pensions I have estimated. One way or another, this will ultimately be recognised in the national accounts – even if it is not recognised today.

I can summarise the likely development of the headline liability value over the next five years by using the data gathered in this study. Figure 5 shows my projection for the likely path of (a) the government's calculations of public sector pension liabilities and (b) my calculations of the public sector pension liabilities. I have assumed that the government will take all of the effect of this year's fall in the discount rate from 3.5 per cent to 2.8 per cent in the one year, which will mean a large rise in their own reported value of liabilities to well over £600 billion. All these estimates assume that the basic terms of the public sector pension schemes remain the same as at the time of writing – in particular that there is no change in the normal retirement age for existing members.[26]

Figure 5   **Future public sector unfunded pension liabilities (£bn)**

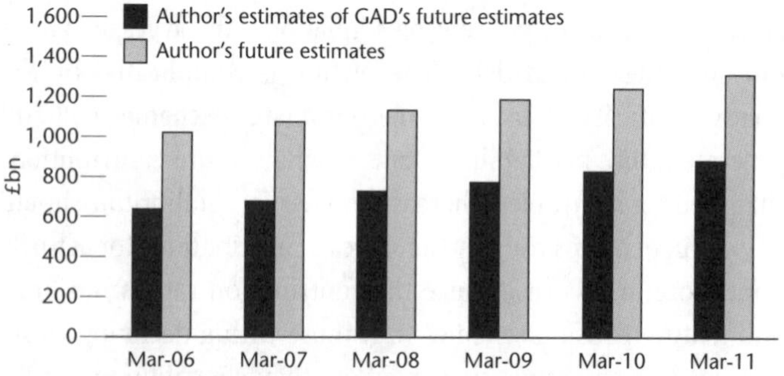

Note: Estimates of future liabilities; constant 1.1% real interest rates assumed; constant 2.8% used for GAD estimates

26 Note that the impact on the path of liabilities of the government's recently announced policy of introducing a 65 retirement age for new entrants is negligible (<1 per cent) over this six-year forecast time span.

Again, these very large numbers in the future are hard to interpret. The same figures can be expressed as a percentage of GDP – and I base GDP forecasts on the average of the last ten years' nominal growth rate of 5.6 per cent less 1 per cent to reflect lower anticipated inflation and growth. Figure 6 illustrates this.

Thus, according to my projections, and assuming no further change to the benefits offered to current public sector employees, the liabilities will be largely stable (rising very slightly) at around 83–85 per cent of GDP. By contrast, the Government Actuary's Department's estimates will continue to rise more rapidly (and particularly next year, when the new discount rate comes into effect) as they continually adjust their assumptions closer to reality. The underlying growth rate is also higher, reflecting the higher-than-market discount rate they have chosen to use.

One caveat should be made, particularly as regards my estimates: the net present value of long-dated liabilities is very

Figure 6 **Future public sector unfunded pension liabilities (estimates of future liabilities; % forecast GDP)**

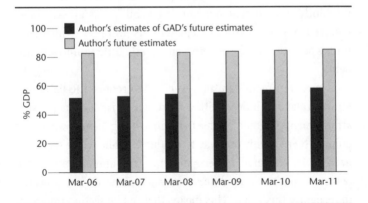

dependent on real interest rates. These future values could vary significantly if real interest rates change markedly either way.

Note that Figures 5 and 6 are not just estimates of the future value of current liabilities, they also assume that all the current schemes continue as at present, accruing current service obligations. So these two graphs are not comparable with the estimates of undiscounted future cash flows in the previous section, which relate only to obligations that the government has already incurred in respect of past service.

Annual cost of pensions

I have concentrated on the headline liability. Knowing this value accurately can do little but scare policy-makers and is unlikely to change the balance of power in negotiations between employers and employees (and their unions). Unless the government changes the way it accounts for its occupational pension liabilities, and includes them in the national debt, then little hangs on the scale of the liabilities except shock headline value. Most relevantly, the current outstanding liability has already been incurred, and apart from reneging on its promises (which later it may have to do), the government can do little to mitigate this debt.

The government can, however, act to reduce the liabilities' growth rate, and indeed with a thorough revision of its pension arrangements it would be able to begin to bring them down. In my opinion there is only one way to do this – public sector *employers* need to be educated to recognise the true annual cost of the pension promise, and public sector *employees* need to be educated to recognise this value. This means that public sector employers need to be charged the full cost of making pension promises to their employees. The greatest barrier to ensuring that employees and employers understand the full cost of the pensions employees are promised is the artificial discount rate that all the schemes still maintain.

Annual cash cost

We can still forecast the expected cash cost of public sector occupational pensions over a longer time frame. This time, I will not assume that the pension schemes continue; instead I will look at what the liability accumulated to date of £1,025 billion looks like in terms of actual cash payment of pensions spread over the future. As this is the liability that has been accumulated to date, very little, if anything, can be done to mitigate it. Figure 7 shows my estimate of future annual public sector occupational pension costs[27] spread over the next 80 years. I assume an inflation rate of 2.95 per cent p.a. over this period. Note that this graph shows only what is *already* committed, not what will become committed for future service.

Real annual cost

We can go back to Chapter 2, and our first-principles methodology, to work out also what pensions are costing not in cash terms, but calculated to include changes in future liabilities, and more particularly expressed as a percentage of individuals' salaries. For this calculation, I go back to the assumption that the schemes continue

---

27 The figures quoted are comparable with the 'Pensions in payment' line in Table B.1 in PESA 2005. The 2004/05 estimated out-turn was £16,525 million.

Figure 7   **Public sector occupational pension payments**

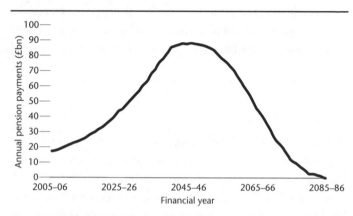

Note: Based on March 2006 liabilities; 2.95% p.a. assumed inflation; £ billion p.a.

in their current form. I will take the five largest schemes – teachers, the NHS, the Civil Service, the armed forces and the police – and for each one calculate the annual cost of the pensions promises to members. I will compare this with the combined employee and employer contribution currently being levied.

I will use a raft of simplifying assumptions for each scheme's cost estimate. In brief:

- Employees work until normal retirement age.
- Employees work sufficient years to earn the maximum normal pension.
- Employees do not buy extra years, or otherwise voluntarily alter the normal entitlements.
- Employees' career paths give rise to average rises above the general salary growth in the economy (2 per cent p.a.) – the

assumed rises are 0.75 per cent p.a. for teachers, NHS and Civil Service staff, and 1.5 per cent p.a. for the police and armed forces.

- The costs are calculated assuming no spouse pension, and no generous ill health and early retirement options. While this is a crude offset, this oversimplification probably compensates for the poor transfer and deferred benefits of the schemes, and for the effect of many employees not serving long enough to qualify for a full pension.

- Female employees do not take sufficient time off work to compromise their pension entitlements.

- Employees continue to pay their current pension contributions.

- Employers are charged the full annual cost (less the employees' contribution) by the pension-paying agencies, assuming these assumptions hold. They will operate under the principle that if they bought index-linked gilts at market prices with these contributions, then they would not accrue either any surplus or any deficit over time.

- Where there is more than one defined-benefit scheme operating the newest one will be used – the one open to new entrants.

- The discount rate used is the market rate.

In reaching the values shown below in Table 12, I have used the methodology from Table 7, adjusted in each case for the specific rules of each scheme. See Table 1 for the summary details of each scheme.

It is clear from the astonishingly high annual cost of these schemes (particularly the police, armed forces and Civil Service)

Table 12 Estimated annual 'real' cost of pensions as a percentage of salary (main unfunded public sector pension schemes, 1.1% real yield, March 2006)

Employer	Employees' contribution (%)	Current employers' contribution (%)	Employees' sex	Author's total calculated cost (%)	Employers' contribution required (%)
Teachers	6.0	13.5	Male	34.7	28.7
			Female	39.0	33.0
NHS	6.0	14.0	Male	34.7	28.7
			Female	39.0	33.0
Civil Service	3.5	13.6	Male	39.5	36.0
			Female	45.3	41.8
Police	11.0	26.0	Male	63.7	52.7
			Female	71.8	60.8
Armed forces	0.0	22.1	Male	49.3	49.3
			Female	54.7	54.7

why the gross liabilities figure is ballooning at such a rate. I do not believe that any of the main employers has any idea that the pensions they offer are costing this much, nor do I believe that ministers are aware of these numbers. Nor do I believe that the Financial Reporting Advisory Board (FRAB – the UK government advisory body that chooses the 'administered' interest rate for calculating these scheme costs) has any idea that the long-term interest rate they have chosen for discounting public sector liabilities has such a material impact on the apparent running costs of these pension schemes.[28]

These values are very sensitive to the real interest rate. Figure 8 shows the elasticity of the annual cost of a $\frac{2}{3}$ final salary index-linked pension with respect to the real interest rate. Note that the values in this graph do not match exactly with the schemes above as it is derived from a stylised pension as shown in Table 7.

In view of the latest, but much criticised, compromise between the government and the unions (October 2005) over pension reform,[29] I have calculated the impact of this reform on the annual

---

28 Note that in arriving at these estimates, I have much less detailed scheme informa-
    tion than that available to the scheme actuaries. I have checked my stylised ver-
    sion of each scheme's liability stream by applying a 3.5 per cent discount rate to
    this stream (as opposed to the market's 1.1 per cent), to see how close the result-
    ant annual contribution level required is to the sum of the current employers'
    and employees' contributions. Subject to the general proviso that males and
    females should be charged a different rate for their pensions, I get close agree-
    ment with the current contribution rates using a 3.5 per cent discount rate for all
    the schemes – in fact I have used this information to ensure that my assumptions
    on career progression for each scheme are as accurate as possible.

29 Which is to raise the normal retirement age from 60 to 65 for new entrants, but to
    maintain the terms for existing employees as they are. It should be noted that there
    was never any intention of changing the value of pension rights already accrued,
    but there were negotiations regarding the accrual of future pension rights for
    existing members (see also the commentaries by Philip Booth and Nick Silver).

Figure 8   **Effect of real interest rate on pension contributions needed**

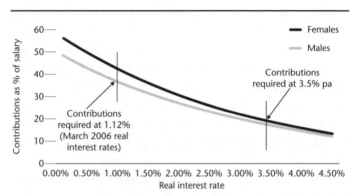

Note: $^2/_3$ final salary index-linked pension at 60; 2% real salary growth; 40 years' contributions; no career progression

cost of pension provision for new employees. Assuming that new entrants work for 45 years up to age 65 (rather than 40 years up to age 60), then the total annual cost of the new pension on the same basis as the calculations above, as a percentage of salary, is, in the case of teachers and the NHS,[30] 30.5 per cent for men (down

---

30 These two schemes are the largest and most representative. The key assumptions are that the accrual rate ($^1/_{80}$th) remains the same at the 65 retirement age, and that the combination of death-in-service and widow's pension promises in practice means that there is no cross-subsidisation of those alive at 65 (and able to draw their pensions) by those dying between 60 and 64. The reader may be intrigued that the reduction in cost is so small. This is because (a) the percentage reduction in life expectancy from 60 to 65 is only 19.2 per cent and 17.9 per cent for males and females respectively (GAD Interim Life Tables, 2001–03), and (b) there is an offset because the annual cost of final salary schemes rises with age, and the extended period of paying into the scheme (45 versus 40 years) means this increases the average cost of the pension (and, of course, its absolute value to the pensioner).

from 34.7 per cent), and 34.8 per cent for women (down from 39.0 per cent). This reduction in the cost of the pension of about 12 per cent is clearly helpful. But given that the accumulated liabilities of new entrants are very low in their early years, the impact on the total growth rate of liabilities is negligible in the near term.

4 POLICY PRESCRIPTIONS –
TRANSPARENCY TO ALL PARTIES

Policy implications

The government deficit for the year to March 2006 is not about 3 per cent p.a. of GDP as will be reported by the Office for National Statistics: it is significantly more. This is because the government is spending (as current account income) money it should be 'investing' for future pensions. Under the current reporting regime, the government will recognise this up to a point. From its *own* numbers, it is incurring occupational pensions costs of £55 billion a year,[1] which it is not recognising. Instead it recognises current pensions in payment (about £18 billion[2]) as a current cost, and since it will receive a little more than that from public sector employers each year (about £21 billion[3] in 2006), it sees the system as financing itself. The 'missing' £34 billion (or 2.8 per cent of GDP), using its own numbers, is the interest cost of the unwinding of the discount rate – i.e. the cost of the pensions being 'unfunded'.[4] So even with these, official, numbers, there is about 3 per cent p.a. of

---

1   Source: Appendix 3, Table 15, sum of rows 3, 5 and 6.

2   Ibid., row 4.

3   Ibid., row 3.

4   In effect the government has spent each year the money that would otherwise have gone into a pension fund, and not reported to anyone that it was doing so, or made any accounting entry anywhere to recognise this fact. So it has built up this huge debt on which it has to pay interest. To call it a 'pension cost' is slightly disingenuous; it is really interest on debt from many previous years' excessive public spending that should really have been curbed to pay for future pensions.

GDP which the government is spending on pensions by making promises to its employees (and therefore being added to government liabilities), which it is not recognising.

But the situation is much worse than this. The 'real' cost of each year's additional service is not £21 billion, but £41 billion.[5] Compound this to the higher absolute value of the pension liability, and even allowing for the lower real rate accrual thereafter, the 'real' spend on public occupational pensions is £76 billion.[6] Since £18 billion is reported as the current pension cost, this leaves an annual gap of £58 billion, or about 4.7 per cent of GDP p.a., which is 'spent' by government on its staff pensions, and which is not reported. This puts the several-hundred-million-pound 'deficit' of the NHS into stark perspective!

What can be done about this enormous problem, which has crept up on us? I think that the following policy changes are necessary:

a) Require an actuarial firm or firms, independent of government, to prepare assumptions that would allow an independent agency to run a solvent funded scheme without

5   The weighted average of the higher rates of contribution from Table 12, i.e. the ratio of £41.1 billion to £20.7 billion, is the same as the ratio of the 'real' annual pensions cost calculated from Table 12 to the actual annual pensions costs charged by the government to the various public sector employers, weighted by their relative sizes.

6   £41.1 billion + (£841 billion x (3.1 per cent + 1.1 per cent)) = £76.4 billion; where £841 billion is the public sector pension liability at market real interest rates as at 31 March 2006, based on £530 billion reported by the government for March 2005, and the already established elasticities; 3.1 per cent is the relevant inflation rate applying to 2005/06, and 1.1 per cent is the real rate of return. The calculation does not include my adjustments for mortality or salary assumptions, nor the accrued service to the year to March 2006 (i.e. the liability is as at March 2005, since that is the 'debt' on which interest will be paid).

the government's guarantee. The fund would be allowed to invest only in UK government securities. This is similar to SCAPE, but using market values, not 'administered' values.

b) Armed with these assumptions, ask the Government Actuary's Department or an independent actuarial firm to calculate the total liability of the public sector schemes, and the ongoing cost to employers. Both these figures will vary with market interest rates.

c) Charge public sector employers the full cost (less the employees' contribution) of pension commitments that they make to their employees.

d) To ensure complete transparency the government could issue new index-linked gilts, and endow a new agency with both the public sector occupational pension liabilities and these new gilts assets. This agency would be required by statute to maintain a near-zero (certainly non-negative) net worth. It would charge the public sector employers accordingly, and buy gilts with the money it received from them.

e) The government may choose to reduce unilaterally some pensions benefits (particularly for new entrants – which it has already done to an extent). This would be the route of choice if, with the new transparency, it became clear that the overall rates of pay in the public sector were above equivalent jobs in the private sector.

f) Finally, we should let the employers negotiate with the workforce over how they wish to split the (now apparently much larger) pension cost. My guess is that the unions (or at least their members) would accept higher basic salaries and lower pension promises and perhaps rather different forms of pension arrangement than those that exist at the moment.

Appendix 1: MAIN UNFUNDED PUBLIC SERVICE PENSION SCHEMES

(Large schemes denoted by bold type)

1 **Armed Forces Pension Scheme**
2 **Principal Civil Service Pension Scheme** (Great Britain)
3 PCSPS (Northern Ireland)
4 **NHS Pension Scheme** (E&W)
5 NHS Pension Scheme (Scotland)
6 Health and Personal Social Services Superannuation Scheme (Northern Ireland)
7 **Teachers' Pension Scheme** (E&W)
8 Scottish Teachers' Superannuation Scheme
9 Northern Ireland Teachers' Superannuation Scheme
10 **Police Pension Scheme** (administered locally by police authorities)
11 Firefighters' Pension Scheme (administered locally by fire and rescue authorities)
12 UK Atomic Energy Authority Pension Scheme
13 Research Councils Pension Scheme
14 Judicial Pension Scheme

Source: GAD

Appendix 2: RECONCILIATION OF ANNUAL CHANGES IN LIABILITIES, 2003–04

In Table 13 below, I reconcile the changes between two adjacent sample years – 2003 and 2004.

Table 13 **Reconciliation of yearly change of unfunded liability, March 2003–March 2004**

		£ billion
1	End-year liabilities, March 2003	425[1]
2	+ PV of new pensions commitments (i.e. pensionable service)	15.5[2]
3	– pensions paid in year	–16.1[3]
4	+ real interest on liabilities (3.5% real in this case)	14.9[4]
5	+ inflation (RPI) (1.7% to September 2002 – triggering April 2003 increases)	7.2[5]
6	Subtotal	446.5
7	**+/– difference between out-turn for 2003/04 and assumptions (i.e. forecasting error)**	**13.5**
8	End-year liabilities, March 2004	460[6]

---

1 Source: GAD.

2 Source: PESA 2005, Table B.1, 'Change in liability', line 2003/04.

3 Source: ibid., 'Pensions in payment', line 2003/04.

4 = 3.5 per cent × £425 billion.

5 = 1.7 per cent × £425 billion. The sum of the interest and inflation charge (= £22.1 billion) reconciles reasonably closely with the 'unwinding of discount rate' line in PESA 2005, Table B1 (£22.5 billion).

6 Source: GAD.

Reconciliation of annual changes in liabilities, 2004–05

Table 14 **Reconciliation of yearly change of unfunded liability, March 2004–March 2005**

		£ billion
1	End-year liabilities, March 2004	460[7]
2	+ PV of new pensions commitments (i.e. pensionable service)	17.5[8]
3	– pensions paid in year	–16.5[9]
4	+ real interest on liabilities (3.5% real in this case)	16.1[10]
5	+ inflation (RPI) (2.8% to September 2003 – triggering April 2004 increases)	12.9[11]
6	Subtotal	490.0
7	**+/– difference between out-turn for 2004/05 and assumptions (i.e. forecasting error)**	**40.0**
8	End-year liabilities, March 2005	530

The £40 billion error term is particularly large in 2004/05 – mainly because of an exceptionally large 'catch-up' following the belated five-year NHS actuarial review and the new discount rate (2.4 per cent p.a.) for the police and fire schemes. In March 2006, HM Treasury issued a reconciliation (presumably based on new – unpublished – PESA 2006 information), which is very similar to this table, with an error term also of £40 billion.

---

7   Source: ibid.

8   Source: PESA 2005, Table B.1, 'Change in liability', line 2004/05.

9   Source: ibid., 'Pensions in payment', line 2004/05.

10 = 3.5 per cent × £460 billion.

11 = 2.8 per cent × £460 billion; 2.8% is the relevant increase in the RPI (September 2003 headline rate). The sum of the interest and inflation charge (= £29 billion) does not reconcile that well with the 'unwinding of the discount rate' line in PESA 2005, Table B1, for 2004/05 (£24.5 billion). Since both the figures I use were known at the date of publication of PESA 2005, this is a mystery.

Appendix 3: FORECAST CHANGE IN LIABILITIES, MARCH 2005–MARCH 2006

Table 15 **Reconciliation of yearly change of unfunded liability, March 2005–March 2006**

		£ billion
1	End-year liabilities, March 2005	530[1]
2	Increase due to change in discount rate	56.3[2]
3	+ PV of new pensions commitments (i.e. pensionable service)	20.7[3]
4	– pensions paid in year	–17.8[4]
5	+ real interest on liabilities (2.8% real in this case)	16.4[5]
6	+ inflation (RPI) (3.1% to September 2004 – triggering April 2005 increases)	18.2[6]
7	Subtotal	623.7
8	+/– forecast error term	15.0
9	End-year liabilities forecast, March 2006	639

The £15 billion error term is my estimate based on historic trends. See text for details.

---

1   Source: GAD.

2   Based on a duration (elasticity) of 18.05 and a real interest rate change of 0.7% (3.5% to 2.8%) applied to 84% of the public sector total – the remainder are the police and fire schemes, which changed their discount rate assumption to 2.4% in the year commencing 1 April 2004, and so are unaffected by this change this year.

3   Source: PESA 2005, Table B.1, 'Change in liability', line 2005/06, Plans.

4   Source: ibid., 'Pensions in payment', line 2005/06, Plans.

5   = 2.8% × (£530 billion + £56.3 billion).

6   = 3.1% × (£530 billion + £56.3 billion); 3.1% is the relevant increase in the RPI (September 2004 headline rate).

COMMENTARY: PUBLIC SECTOR PENSION REFORM
Philip Booth[1]

Introduction

Neil Record has done a remarkable job in revealing the true liabilities and future costs of public sector pension schemes. He has suggested various measures to improve transparency so that decision-making in the future can be more responsible. It is the purpose of this commentary to discuss further the policy implications of the author's work.

This problem has been discussed wholly in connection with the UK. Many other countries, however, suffer from similar problems. Sin (2001), writing for the World Bank, states:

> Although there are instances of funded schemes with a portion of their revenue derived from investment income, the State is still not exempt from carrying any shortfall that arises. This situation is likely to drain government coffers even more as these schemes mature. The impact of the rapid increase in pension costs will be most keenly felt when policy directions towards reducing expenditure and restoring fiscal balance put government budgets under strain.

---

1   Philip Booth is Professor of Insurance and Risk Management at the Sir John Cass Business School, City University, and Editorial and Programme Director at the Institute of Economic Affairs. He is also a Fellow of the Institute of Actuaries and of the Royal Statistical Society and has worked at the Bank of England as an adviser on financial stability matters.

The particular characteristics of the UK schemes are also typical around the world, with the vast majority not being pre-funded, according to Sin. Reform is, however, taking place in a few countries. In some cases this involves reducing benefits in various ways (for example, in Italy, Brazil, Greece and Portugal); in other cases contributions are being required from employees where they were not previously required (for example, in South Korea). The USA has introduced fully funded defined-contribution schemes for new employees.[2] Certain government agencies in the UK, such as the regulators Ofcom and the FSA, have also introduced defined-contribution schemes. The UK government needs to undertake radical reform if it is not to increase this hidden debt that it is leaving to future generations.

The nature of the problem

Neil Record has spelt out, in stark terms, the nature of the problem. Pensions have been promised to public sector employees, yet no fund has been accumulated to meet future pension obligations, except in the case of local government employees. Nevertheless, there is an implicit, if not explicit, contractual guarantee between the government and its employees. Thus there is a very real burden of debt, placed on the shoulders of future taxpayers. The liability will be borne by future taxpayers and the corresponding beneficiaries are current public sector workers. The nature of the public sector pension schemes also discourages the mobility between the public and private sectors that the government is trying to

2   See http://www.frtib.gov/.

encourage, as benefits for early leavers are almost always worth less than benefits for those who remain in the schemes.

Other than the policies to promote transparency that Neil Record has already proposed, we can examine three possible forms of policy option.

The first approach would be to find ways to reduce the debt burden by reducing the value of pension promises already made to current workers. In effect this would involve breaking contracts. This option should not necessarily be ruled out – there are occasions, *in extremis*, when two parties agree to reduce the obligations of one towards the other if those obligations become overwhelming.[3] From a moral perspective, this approach would be similar to the government reneging on national debt payments or deliberately reducing the value of its debt by inflation. From an economic perspective, such a move would also be damaging. The credibility of the government as an employer would be reduced in the eyes of employees and potential employees because they would not trust the government to keep promises that were made to them. As a result workers might demand higher wages, as they might feel that their pension benefits were insecure. If that happened, cost savings would be dissipated. This is very similar to the effect of interest rates rising if the government's inflation or debt repayment policy becomes less credible. This approach is a last resort and we therefore do not investigate it further.

The second series of options would involve changing the existing pension arrangements for all current employees as well as new employees – in other words stop future pension accrual and move to a new type of pension arrangement. This would involve

---

3   For example, when rescheduling corporate or government debt repayments.

tough negotiations with employees because the value of the benefit package going forward would change.

The third series of options would involve making new pension arrangements for all new entrants to the various public sector labour forces, but allowing existing members to remain in their current schemes. This has the advantage of not changing arrangements for current employees, but has the disadvantage of potentially giving rise to a 'two-class' workforce – one with new pension arrangements and one with old pension arrangements. The other disadvantage is that any reduction in the accumulation of new pension liabilities will happen very slowly. It is worth noting, however, that many companies in the private sector are taking this approach.

Changing future arrangements: raising retirement age

Government proposals
The government proposed changing the rules for future pension accrual in June 2003 and withdrew these proposals before the 2005 general election. Proposals for different types of public sector workers varied. The main approach involved raising retirement ages. In the case of civil servants and NHS workers (but not teachers) proposals were also made to move to a career-average benefit.[4] Under these proposals, existing accrued benefits would

---

4 Current government schemes pay pensions that are based on an employee's final salary at the time of retirement. Career-average schemes involve basing the pension on the average salary over the time of service (with some form of up-rating of each year's salary up to the time of retirement being necessary before averaging). Clearly the final salary scheme benefits those whose salary rises quickly just before retirement and those who stay in the scheme until the time of their retirement.

have been preserved. But, from the changeover time (originally proposed as 2013), all new pension accrued would be payable from age 65. The affected workers could choose to take their pension from any age, subject to their contract and other legislation, but, if they retired before 65, the pension accrued after 2013 would be actuarially adjusted downwards.

New entrants to the government payroll would be admitted into the pension scheme on the basis that their accrued pension rights would be based on a retirement age of 65.

Analysis of government pre-election proposals

The proposals would have done nothing to reduce the existing accrued debt. As explained above, such action may indeed be inappropriate. The proposals would, of course, have reduced the rate at which future debt would accrue. If we ignore the transition period and consider only the proposals to raise the retirement age, the effect of this proposal can be seen by examining the difference between the cost of accruing a year's pension with a retirement age of 65 and the cost of accruing a year's pension under the current rules, with a retirement age of 60. That difference in cost, as an average percentage of payroll, would be about 5 per cent, assuming that in each case the accrual rate (say $\frac{1}{80}$th) was the same. This would have represented an effective pay cut for relevant public sector workers.

There were two major drawbacks to the government's 2003 proposals. The first is that new workers would have been treated differently from existing workers until 2013. The second, more serious, problem is that it does not change anything in principle. New pension debts will still be accumulated; unless the other recommendations of this monograph are taken on board, the cost of those pensions (and the value of them to public sector workers) will still be opaque. There will be a reduction in the value of the pension benefit aspect of the remuneration package, but, as life expectancy continues to rise, the problems we have at present, with ever-rising public sector pension deficits, will resurface.

Combining a rise in the retirement age with a move to a career-average scheme would, though, have removed one of the more pernicious aspects of the current schemes. When public sector pay awards are given, this does, of course, lead to a considerable increase in the current cost of employing public sector workers. This is well understood and transparent and would be taken into account in negotiations between the government and employees. It is much less well understood that, because public sector pensions are based on salaries at retirement, an increase in salaries (say by 10 per cent) would lead the whole of the past accumulated pension liability, including the pension rights accumulated as a result of all past service, to increase by approximately 10 per cent too.[5] If there were a move towards a career-average scheme, an increase in salaries in any one year would have a much less significant effect on the total accumulated pension liability.[6] Nevertheless, even the more radical government proposals did far too little to promote transparency and, hence, rational decision-making for employers, employees and taxpayers.

---

5 The increase would not be exactly 10 per cent for various technical reasons.
6 Because the pension is based on an employee's average salary (uprated for inflation) over their working life.

Government climb-down

More recently the government has agreed with public sector unions that reforms designed to reduce costs will only apply to new entrants to the schemes. The watered-down proposals will mean that the future accrual of public sector pension debts will continue at a barely unchanged rate for many years to come. It also requires new entrants to the workforce to work under different terms and conditions of employment from existing employees. This has, of course, happened in the private sector too. All the problems of public sector schemes – poor governance leading to high ill-health retirement, lack of transparency of costs and so on – will remain.

Proposals to change future arrangements: development of defined-contribution schemes

A sharp break from the current arrangements could be achieved by moving to a defined-contribution pension scheme for public sector workers. This approach is being taken in many private sector companies and, as has been noted, is also a feature of public sector pension reform elsewhere. Defined-benefit schemes of the kind that exist in the public sector are becoming very rare in the private sector. Some autonomous government agencies have moved towards defined-contribution arrangements too, including the Financial Services Authority. If, however, other public sector employers replace existing defined-benefit arrangements with defined-contribution arrangements, many potential issues still need to be resolved. Specifically, these are:

- Should the change apply just to new entrants or also to existing workers?

- How are other aspects of the pay package changed to reflect reductions in the value of pension benefits?
- How should a defined-contribution scheme be administered?

Each of these issues will be taken in turn. The first issue is, of course, the same issue that the government has been trying to grapple with in its reform of public sector schemes. They are also the same issues, of course, that any private sector employer has to take into account when revising their pension arrangements. It may be possible to have a more effective resolution of these problems if the government is willing to compensate for loss of pension schemes by increased pay.

Should existing workers be affected?

In my view, all workers in the public sector should be treated the same way, as far as their benefits package is concerned. It is untenable to have new entrants to the workforce on a much higher basic level of pay but with a much smaller pension benefit than existing workers. This problem would be exacerbated because of the way the cost of accruing a year's pension in a defined-benefit scheme varies with age and also sex, so that any pay adjustment designed to compensate for the loss of a pension benefit might have to vary with age (see also below). I favour the complete cessation of all defined-benefit accrual within public sector schemes, an appropriate adjustment to salaries and the development of a defined-contribution pension scheme for public sector workers.

How should the remuneration package be affected?

Neil Record suggests in this monograph that the accumulation of public sector pension debts be made explicit in the future by increasing the budget for government salaries and charging government departments for the cost of accrued pension benefits. He further suggests that a fund of index-linked gilts should be accumulated to back future pension promises. Thus the proposals in the main part of the monograph will see a considerable increase in the explicit cost of public sector worker remuneration as the cost of their pensions schemes is made explicit. If the right to accrual of new benefits within those schemes is withdrawn, then the cost of accruing benefits (35 per cent of salary on average for male teachers and NHS workers, for example; 39 per cent of salary for females) would be available for enhancing salary packages in other ways. Precisely how the benefits package would be changed would be a matter for negotiation. It is likely, however, that it could be enhanced to provide as valuable a deal for employees at a reduced cost to the government, because employees would receive a greater proportion of their remuneration package in cash. Cash is normally more valuable than a benefit in kind of equivalent cost.

The government could keep back a proportion of the cash that would otherwise be available for a salary enhancement to make what would, in effect, be compulsory contributions into a defined-contribution pension scheme (for example, 5 per cent of salary). Alternatively, it could match employees' contributions up to a certain level. The government, as employer, could also provide certain forms of insurance, some of which are provided by defined-benefit pension schemes and not by defined-contribution schemes (for example, life insurance and widow/widower benefits), as well as other insurances that might be of value (such as permanent health insurance, critical-illness insurance and disability insurance) where these are not already provided. The government, in its role as employer, may be able to obtain these insurances more cheaply than individual employees and without underwriting.

In any negotiations, there would be one extremely difficult issue to be addressed. How should any salary enhancements vary with age and sex? The cost of financing a year's accrual of defined-benefit pension varies with age and also between males and females. If a uniform increase in salaries were offered in compensation for the loss of the defined-benefit pension scheme, males would gain at the expense of females.[7] The value of a salary enhancement relative to the value of the pension scheme will vary with age but not in a straightforward way. This problem can be alleviated by creating greater competition in the provision of public services, as that would ensure that overall salaries simply reflect market rates (see below), but this more radical solution takes us beyond the realm of pension reform. All we can say at this stage is that it is necessary for the government to negotiate pay scales that reflect the value of employees of different ages and levels of experience (as well as talent). Pension reform may have to take place in conjunction with the complete renegotiation of public sector pay and conditions. Radical renegotiation of salary packages might not, however, be as difficult as it may appear at first sight. All employees would have the potential for considerable salary enhancements in cash terms.

---

7   Although this could be regarded as putting right the discrimination that exists against men in defined-benefit pension schemes – benefits for women are of greater value because of their higher life expectancy: defined-benefit pension schemes finance a longer expected retirement for women from a given length of working life.

The issue of special retirement ages in certain public sector schemes (police, armed forces and the fire brigade) would also dissolve if the approach to pension reform suggested here were adopted. These pension schemes are particularly costly. Employees would therefore receive considerable salary enhancements upon their defined-benefit schemes being closed, even if the cash enhancement were scaled down below the value of the former pension benefit. If these employees wished to use the cash enhancement to their salaries to invest very large amounts in defined-contribution pension funds to facilitate early retirement, that would be a matter for the individual employee. It is quite likely, given the employment opportunities available to former police and fire staff, that they would, in fact, prefer a higher level of 'take-home' pay and then continue to work in other sectors after they had retired from the emergency services.

The administration of public sector defined-contribution schemes
If the contribution to a public sector defined-contribution pension scheme were 10 per cent of salary, on average, the total contribution in 2005 would have been about £10 billion. Those who value liberal markets would be concerned about investment decisions relating to this amount of capital being effectively controlled by the government. In the long term, the government could control about 15 per cent of all funds invested in securities through funded, defined-contribution, public sector pension schemes. It is important that governance procedures in pension funds are developed to prevent this degree of government power over capital markets from becoming a problem.

There are several ways this problem could be avoided, and only one way is suggested here. Rather than the government controlling or contracting a fund manager to run a public sector pension fund, each individual employee should be free to choose any defined-contribution or stakeholder pension scheme. Both the employer and employee contributions would be invested in the nominated scheme. Such a mechanism might be more costly than one large administered fund, but it need not be. One would expect public sector trade unions to join with fund managers and other pension providers to provide a standard product that would be suitable and acceptable to many public sector workers. If this were done, most of the benefits of economies of scale in investment and administration should still be reaped. In the author's view the government should have nothing to do with the investment and administration of pension funds – even those for its own employees. This would be, nevertheless, a legitimate role for trade unions, as would be the provision of financial advice.

Would 'opting out' be possible?

One approach to reform, which would involve a degree of voluntarism that might be more acceptable to public service employees, would be a mechanism of 'opting out'. Employees who preferred to remain in the current system could forgo the considerable pay rise made to those who chose to make their own defined-contribution pension arrangements. With the current public sector schemes, such an approach would be problematic. The defined-benefit pension, based on salary at retirement, has a value that differs over the age range and which varies between the sexes. Employees could opt in and out at times that gave them the greatest financial advantage. A further problem is that, if there is an unexpected rise in general salaries, those who are near retirement and who remain in the current pension scheme obtain a windfall gain, in that the pension based on the whole of their service to date will increase in line with the salary increase.

The government could, however, establish a career-average scheme (with a retirement age of 65 and optional membership). As has been noted, the government has been attracted to the career-average model. It is easier to envisage allowing employees to join or leave such a scheme at will. Joining would be in return for a contribution equal to the actuarial cost of accruing benefit in the scheme in any given year of service. The contribution would still vary with age, but the costs of funding a career-average scheme are much more predictable than the costs of funding a given year's pension entitlement in a scheme in which the pension is based on salary at retirement, and thus an appropriate contribution for those who chose to join the scheme would be much easier to calculate.[8]

Wider public service reform

It is worth considering pension reform in the context of wider public service reform.

There have been tentative moves to give individual hospitals more control over the pay and conditions for their workers. For

---

8   The arrangements for contracting out of S2P/SERPS (the state's earnings-related pension scheme open to all employed people) involve the payment of a National Insurance rebate to those who are contracted out. The S2P scheme is a form of career-average scheme and the National Insurance rebates, which are supposed to be equal to the value of the pension somebody forgoes by not being in the scheme, are not difficult to calculate in principle (although they are widely regarded as being too low).

example, Foundation Hospitals are able to vary pay and conditions from national agreements. A wider agenda for public service reform should allow all schools and hospitals to determine their own pay and conditions. The freedom to pursue their own pension arrangements should be part of that process of giving autonomy to schools and hospitals. Schools and hospitals may wish to recombine for the purpose of certain aspects of negotiations (for example, the Catholic Church may wish to negotiate pay and conditions for teachers and other workers within Catholic Voluntary Aided schools). This would, however, be a matter for the institutions concerned. Different combinations of pay and other benefits may well then become common in different parts of the country.

Crucially, the pension arrangements, as well as other aspects of the remuneration package, would be determined independently by individual schools and hospitals. They could buy into insured defined-benefit schemes if they wished (including a possible career-average scheme described above), or schools and hospitals could group together (as universities have) to run their own defined-benefit or defined-contribution schemes. The grants to schools and hospitals would not, however, depend on the cost of the benefit packages they offered or on the number or age of employees – individual employers would be wholly responsible for determining those.

Clearly this approach could not be applied to the Civil Service and the armed forces (although it could be applied to the police). But in the areas of health and education it would be compatible with wider public service reform that involved giving the purchasing power to individuals to obtain health and education from government or from alternative private sector providers.

Conclusion

Neil Record has shown how, silently, public sector pension debts have crept up on the taxpayer. He is right to state that the first step in reform is to make these debts explicit. The second step is to make the cost of defined-benefit pensions an explicit part of the salary package. Once this has been done, radical reform should be possible that would benefit everybody – taxpayers and public sector workers alike. Wider reform would particularly benefit younger public sector workers. Older workers may well have adjusted their spending patterns, work patterns and retirement plans to the particular form of public sector pension provision. But new entrants to teaching, nursing and so on should have greater freedom, and would, no doubt, value greater freedom, with regard to the composition of their remuneration package. If this greater freedom can be combined with a more general agenda for public service reform, one that gives greater independence to providers of services and greater freedom to customers, a great service will have been done to both consumers and producers of public services.

COMMENTARY: THE UNNECESSARY BURDEN OF PUBLIC SECTOR PENSION SCHEMES

Nick Silver[1]

Neil Record has estimated the total cost and liability of public sector pension schemes on a realistic basis. While commentators have disagreed over the exact figures, there is a consensus that the size of the liabilities far exceeds official estimates and is considerably larger than the entire official national debt.

The fact that the UK's national debt, including pension liabilities, is over 3 times higher than official estimates is self-evidently important. Without drastic measures, however, not that much can be done about the accrued liability as it has already been incurred. Neil Record also shows that the liabilities are increasing at an alarming rate. The small and inadequate attempts that the government has made to control these costs have foundered on strong union resistance.

I shall argue that this is not surprising given the schemes' governance structure. I also argue that owing to the incidence of tax, the actual cost of the schemes to the taxpayer is even higher than Neil Record's estimates suggest; much of the incurred cost is unnecessary and a waste of money.

---

1   Nick Silver is a Fellow of the Institute of Actuaries and specialises in pension policy reform. He is currently advising the Republic of Macedonia on pension reform. He has previously advised the governments of Bosnia and Herzegovina and the Bank of Uganda. He has published a research paper for the Pensions Policy Institute on the reform of UK public sector pension schemes.

This leads to a radical solution through giving a choice of remuneration packages to public sector workers, which would be both cheaper and more popular than other proposed reforms.

Uncontrolled costs caused by a failure of governance

How did the large and escalating costs of public sector schemes come about, and what lessons do they provide for us? A comparison with what has happened to private sector schemes provides many of the answers to this question (see Table 16).

Table 16 **Assets and liabilities of final salary pension schemes in 2005**

	Public sector[2]	Private sector[3]
Liabilities (£ billion)	1,025	1,070
Assets (£ billion)	0	630
Number of members (million)[4]	6.7	14.9

Table 16 indicates that public sector schemes have a higher liability per person, reflecting better benefits in those schemes.

A more important difference is that private sector schemes are mostly closed to new entrants, so future costs will gradually reduce. Also, the private sector pension promises are backed by £630 billion of assets so that private sector schemes only have a 'shortfall' of £440 billion.

The key question is why have most private sector schemes closed when public sector schemes have not changed at all?

---

2   From Table 11.

3   UBS (2005). Liability has been adjusted by the same interest rate factor as Table 11, namely + 40.8% of 760.

4   Including active members, deferred members and pensioners.

The major difference between the sectors is in their govern-ance. Both private and public sector employers have an incent-ive not to reform or to close their pension schemes, first because it inevitably causes trouble with the workforce, and second because the senior management usually have generous final salary pensions. As I shall explain, the closure of the private sector schemes was caused by a large increase in both real and apparent cost. The real cost increase also happened in the public sector, but there are inherent reasons why this has not led to change.

In the private sector, company managers have incentives to maximise shareholder value. If they do not do so, this is shown up quickly through annual accounts and the company could be taken over and/or management lose their jobs. Management act as agents for shareholders. They do not always act in share-holders' best interests but there are strong forces pulling them in that direction.

In contrast, public sector employers act as agents for taxpayers. The government is subject to direct discipline only by a five-yearly election, in which the public vote on many important issues other than pension costs. The government is also subject to indirect discipline via media scrutiny, but again this is wrapped up with many other issues. Also, those who manage pension matters are the ultimate employers (for example, the NHS or hospital trusts, the army, police authorities and so on). The accountability of these bodies to the electorate, who bear the cost of their deci-sions, is very tenuous indeed.

The different nature of the employers cannot be changed. There are, however, other differences between the private and public sectors which have blocked reform in the public sector.

Private sector costs have increased by more, the feedback to private sector employers is greater and has dramatically increased, and opposition to change is greater in the public sector.

The costs of all final salary schemes have increased owing to a change in financial conditions – specifically lower inflation and interest rates, and mortality improvements. Additionally, private sector schemes have been subject to a large amount of regulatory interference guaranteeing benefits and generally increasing costs. Public sector schemes either already guaranteed these benefits (for example, pensions in payment have been inflation-linked for some time) or have not been subject to the same regulation as private sector schemes. The result is that the cost of private sector schemes has *increased* by more than that of public sector schemes, even though the cost of the latter remains higher.

Probably the main cause of the closures of private sector schemes is the effectiveness of and recent change in the feedback mechanism to decision-makers within the sponsoring employer. Actuarial valuations are triennial, as opposed to being quinquennial[5] in the public sector, ensuring that costs are more regularly communicated to the employer. More significant was the introduction of a new accounting standard for pension costs, FRS17. This means that pension deficits are included on company balance sheets at market values. Disclosure in itself had little impact, but once the disclosure became meaningful – the deficit is now like any other company debt and hence affects the value of the

---

5   Recent public sector valuations have been delayed even beyond five years.

company – action became rapid, with the majority of companies closing schemes to new entrants.

The third reason why public sector schemes have not closed is the strength of opposition to pensions reform by public sector unions, which have been militantly opposed to any change, even when cost-neutral, while government has nearly always backed down from reform. In the private sector, this has not happened to such an extent.

As explained above, the public sector employers are less motivated to force through changes than private sector employers. In addition, the poor public sector governance structure and lack of transparency make opposition to change more likely – unions are aware of the spiralling costs and liabilities of the schemes, which represent a valuable benefit to members. As the schemes do not have the protection of the private sector's governance systems, such as independent trustees and pre-funding, the power to change lies with the government, which has an incentive to try to reduce costs and hence benefits. Aware of this, unions must therefore make a strong show of force at the time of every proposed reform.

From the government's perspective, they have powerful union groups opposing any change, but there exists no vocal, concentrated interest group that will benefit from the change; worse, the costs of the schemes will not be incurred until after the current generation of politicians and taxpayers have retired, so the main beneficiary of reform will be future taxpayers and politicians, who have no voice. Unions also quite rightly highlight the fact that MPs have the most generous pension of all (see Table 17), which undermines both the government's moral case and desire for reform.

Table 17 **MPs' pensions compared with typical pension schemes**

	MPs' pension scheme	Typical public sector scheme	Typical private sector scheme
Benefits on retirement	Based on service with pension of $^1/_{40}$th salary for each year of service	Based on service with pension of $^1/_{80}$th of salary for each year of service plus lump sum	Based on service with pension of $^1/_{60}$th of salary for each year of service
Approximate cost (% of salary)	50%	32–36%	25%

A simple solution to structural problems

A partial solution to the problems of public sector pensions would, therefore, be for the government to apply the rules it applies to private sector employers to its own pension schemes, namely:

1 *Triennial valuations:* in the time since the last public sector valuations, there have been dramatic changes; a substantial deterioration (from pension schemes' perspective) of financial conditions; improved life expectancy; a large increase in the number and pay of public sector workers; and a change in actuarial methodology. The result is that both actual and recorded costs of the schemes have substantially increased and have been previously underestimated. There is no apparent justification for quinquennial valuations.

2 *Independent trustees:* the government is the only employer that has total control of its employees' pension schemes. It is not clear why this should be so. Introducing trustees would start to partially allay union suspicion; would make valuations

more prompt (as trustees have a statutory responsibility to provide regular valuations); would make costs transparent (trustees would be responsible for collecting employer contributions); and would improve governance, which could lead to a reduction in costs.

3 *Meaningful disclosure:* in the private sector, the disclosure of deficits on company balance sheets gave companies the impetus to take action. Public sector liabilities are (inaccurately) disclosed, but not in a way that gives the government incentives to take them seriously. They must therefore be included as part of the national debt, akin to private sector schemes, and actual scheme contribution rates as set by the independent trustees must be included in overall government spending.

It would be naive to suggest that if these measures were introduced, unions would drop all opposition to reforms. There has been recent opposition to changes proposed by BG PLC and to the Local Government Schemes; the former is a private sector scheme and the latter are funded with similar governance structures to those in private sector. Introducing a governance structure similar to that used in private sector schemes would, however, make the costs explicit and introduce an independent body (namely the trustees) with specific responsibility for the management of the schemes, ensuring regular cost updates and accurate contribution collection. This would both motivate the government into action by causing the schemes' true cost and liabilities to directly affect government budgeting, and start to reassure unions that the schemes are no longer under the arbitrary control of the government as employer.

Ill-health retirement

An example of poor governance leading to unnecessarily excessive costs is the high rate of early retirements through ill health in public sector schemes, costing the taxpayer £1 billion per annum.

Public sector schemes have generous benefits for members who retire early owing to ill health (HMT, 2000). Typically, if a member is allowed to retire early owing to ill health, he or she receives an enhanced pension paid immediately. This represents a cost over and above the normal cost for a scheme because (i) the level of benefit paid is higher than the accrued pension and (ii) the pension is paid for longer than expected.

Many private sector schemes also have generous ill-health benefits, but the main difference between the public and private sectors is the higher incidence of ill-health retirement in the public sector (ibid.) – in most private sector schemes only a few exceptional cases receive ill-health pensions, whereas in some public sector schemes it has almost become the norm (see Table 18).

Table 18 **Incidence of ill-health retirement**

	Ill-health retirement as % of all retirements, average 1995–2000
Fire	68
Police	49
Local government	39
NHS	23
Teachers	25
Civil Service	22
Armed forces	6
Private sector	<20

The high rate of ill-health retirement is estimated to cost the government £1 billion a year (ibid.). It should be noted that ill-health retirement is much lower in the private sector *despite* a higher normal retirement age.

Table 18 shows that not only is the number of early retirements due to ill health much higher in the public sector, but there is a large difference between public sector schemes: the fire and police schemes having particularly high rates. These schemes are exceptional in two ways. First they require a degree of physical fitness to undertake employment. Therefore someone who is physically not capable of being a policeman or fireman owing to ill health may be physically capable of doing many other jobs. Second there is even slacker governance of these schemes than in other public sector schemes: local police and fire authorities are responsible for scheme administration, collecting contributions and paying pensions (PPI, 2005).

As far as pensions costs are concerned, these two factors have produced a lethal combination: employees have established a de facto right to ill-health retirement when they can no longer perform their jobs, even though they would be capable of other work. The employer who authorises the retirement does not have to bear the cost, as it will fall as a current cost under future employers' budgets when the pension is actually paid. In other words, unlike in the private sector, if a decision is taken to provide an enhanced pension owing to ill-health retirement, the cost of that decision is not recognised when the decision is taken but over a number of years as the pension is paid.

The best solution to this problem would be to introduce independent trustees, who would require the employer to pay the considerable excess cost of ill-health retirements. This would mean that employers would be much more reluctant to grant ill-health retirements, and would be forced to take more cost-effective measures, such as retraining employees for other work or taking other action to look after the health of their employees. The employers could also take out private insurance against any costs of ill-health retirement and the insurance company would then be required (and have the incentive) to police ill-health retirements.

To fund or not to fund?

It could be argued that liabilities are not a problem in a pay-as-you-go system. Public sector schemes have been around for a long time (since 1810), so should be in a steady state. While today's active members do not have their benefits financed by today's taxpayers, the pensions of previous years' active members are paid for by today's taxpayers. Future taxpayers will then be paying for the pensions of our generation of public sector employees, while not paying for their own, and so on. The tax base grows as the economy grows, so the government can more easily pay the pensions of former civil servants, so the argument goes.

As Neil Record has shown, the problem with this argument is that the schemes' costs are continually increasing, making the pay-as-you-go system akin to pyramid selling. The rate of the increase in liabilities has been approximately 7 per cent per annum over the last seven years, far in excess of GDP growth. Furthermore, we are entering unknown territory for government revenue owing to the decline in the dependency ratio caused by the ageing population. The costs and liabilities of the schemes have become a significant and rising portion of the government's budget and debt, and should be properly recognised. It is not even a debt that can be inflated away – a typical last resort of governments – as pensions are linked to inflation.

A case for funding is that the increases in asset values can often outpace the increase in liabilities and therefore the ultimate amount that employers have to pay into schemes will be reduced. Neil Record argues that this can be accomplished only by taking risks. Recent research has shown, however, that pension liabilities cannot be matched with risk-free assets owing to inherent background risk (Cardinale et al., 2005) (i.e. owing to mortality and labour risks) and hence the 'safest' investment is indeed a diversified portfolio of equities. In the long term, equity values have increased approximately in line with GDP.[6]

Whether funding is cheaper is open to debate. Only accurate funding, however, provides the discipline required to control costs. In theory, an unfunded scheme can be governed as well and as transparently as a funded scheme. This has clearly not happened in practice, despite attempts to do so. Actual money has to change hands before costs are recognised – otherwise all parties involved have vested interests in sweeping the costs under the carpet.

It has been suggested, including by Neil Record, that the schemes should be completely funded by government bonds. This is probably not viable – a government auction of £1 billion of bonds would have serious and unforeseeable effects on the financial markets, even if an equivalent value of the bonds were held by the schemes concerned. It will also not solve the discipline problem as the costs are mostly sunken; there is not much the government can now do to alter the costs of commitments that have already been made.

---

6   Both the return on pension fund investment and a government's ability to pay will be affected by a myriad of other factors, making the cost-effectiveness or otherwise of funding ambiguous.

A more realistic solution would be to fund new liabilities. Accrued liabilities to date could then be made an explicit debt from the government to the schemes' trustees. In effect the accrued debt would be backed by non-tradable government bonds.

Value for money?

The argument could be made that though public sector schemes are expensive, they are affordable and they provide gold-standard benefits. They do not, however, represent value for money.

From an employer's point of view, there are two main reasons for having a pension plan: one is economic, the other paternalistic. The first reason is to attract and retain employees. As a corollary it can be cheaper for employers to provide pensions, rather than individual employees providing them, because of economies of scale and the diversification of risk. The second, more paternalistic, reason is so that ex-employees are looked after when they retire.[7] Schemes were originally set up for such paternalistic reasons; the concept is now antiquated, however, especially with a widely available alternative in the form of private savings vehicles.

The first reason for pension schemes still holds – pension schemes are generally popular with employees, and therefore do perform the function of attracting and retaining employees. At what cost, however, is this achieved? Is there a more cost-effective alternative? In this section I will argue that the cost is far too high and that there is an alternative that is both cheaper and will better attract and retain staff.

---

7   'In England it is generally understood to mean pay given to a state hireling for treason to his country'; Dr Johnson's definition of state pensions for public servants in his dictionary of 1755 (Rhodes, 1965).

Current public sector pension provision is far more generous than that offered in the private sector. Most employees in the public sector are entitled to a pension, whereas most are not in the private sector. Of those who are entitled to a pension in the private sector, the majority can join only a defined-contribution scheme. In the public sector, employees can join a far more valuable final salary scheme. The final salary schemes in the public sector are more generous than those in the private sector. There is no discernible difference in pay and other benefits between the two sectors, except at the highest level (PPI, 2005). The conclusion must be that the public sector schemes are more generous than are required to attract and retain staff from the private sector.

Neil Record has shown that the actual cost of providing scheme benefits is surprisingly high: much higher than employers themselves advertise, and also much higher than employees might reasonably expect. This means that employees are effectively being paid far more than they think they are – if pensions schemes are designed to attract and retain staff, the difference between actual cost and perceived value is a waste of money.

Using the market as a guide to the true value to employers, final salary schemes are too expensive and incur greater risks than financiers are willing to bear. The proof of this is the private sector's decision to close schemes; in the opinion of the private sector, final salary schemes are not economically viable or have risks attached that are too great. The more expensive public sector schemes must therefore be even less economically viable. In addition, taxpayers are bearing risks that shareholders of private companies are increasingly choosing not to bear.

So far, the discussion has not taken tax into account. A key issue with pensions is that they benefit from certain tax exemptions:

- employer and employee contributions are tax exempt and receive National Insurance relief;
- investment returns on funds are tax exempt;[8]
- certain benefits are tax free, for example cash lump sums on retirement.

Surely tax is not important for unfunded public sector schemes? In fact it is crucial. All things being equal, would I, as a taxpayer, prefer a teacher to be paid a pension or the same value in salary (e.g. 28.7 per cent[9] for a male, as calculated by Neil Record)? I would rather the teacher were paid extra salary, because the teacher will have to pay tax and National Insurance on this salary, thus increasing the government's income and hence ultimately reducing my tax bill.

This is in contrast to a private sector employer who has more inclination to remunerate employees through pension as the employer and/or employee receives favourable tax treatment: employer contributions and investment returns are tax exempt. Depending on one's view of the appropriate tax base, this could

---

8   Though this is no longer true of returns from equity investments.

9   This analysis ignores employees' own contributions. On the one hand, employees do not pay tax and National Insurance on their contributions and thus they could be included in the figures. On the other hand, public sector employees would, no doubt, choose to invest something in pensions vehicles, even if their defined-benefit schemes were closed – just like private sector employees, they would then receive tax relief on those contributions (though they would still pay National Insurance).

be regarded as a government subsidy to the tune of £12 billion (Pensions Commission, 2005).

There are two important implications of this. First, the private sector is abandoning final salary schemes as they are too expensive, even with a favourable tax regime, whereas the public sector is persisting with more expensive schemes despite unfavourable tax implications for the taxpayers who bear the ultimate liability. Second, the cost to the taxpayer of public sector schemes is even higher than Neil Record has calculated (see Table 19).

Table 19 **Annual cost of pensions as percentage of salary[10]**

	Cost to the taxpayer of the employers' contribution (%)		
Employer	No allowance for tax[11]	Basic-rate taxpayer[12]	Higher-rate taxpayer[13]
Teachers	28.7	39.1	44.3
NHS	28.7	39.1	44.3
Civil Service	36	47.9	53.8
Police	52.7	71.8	81.4
Armed forces	49.3	64.1	71.5

This table is remarkable in that it shows, for example, that police officers are effectively being paid almost double their salary owing to pension contributions.[14] This is the cost of providing a pension rather than a salary to a policeman who pays higher-rate

10   For simplicity, males only are shown.

11   Table 7, this volume.

12   To calculate this column, the total cost calculated in Table 7 has been increased by 30 per cent (basic-rate tax plus allowance for NI rebates), and then employee contributions deducted.

13   To calculate this column, the total cost calculated in Table 7 has been increased by 45 per cent (higher-rate tax plus allowance for NI rebates), and then employee contributions deducted.

14   Table 19 ignores the exceedingly high ill-health retirement rates shown in Table 18, which will make the effective extra pay even higher.

tax. If salary were paid to a policeman equal to the percentage indicated in the fourth column of Table 19, then that salary would have the same cost to the taxpayer as paying for the pension rights that the policeman accrues. The discrepancy between the figures in the third and fourth columns and those in the second column arises because if the salary were paid the policeman would pay tax and the employer National Insurance on the salary, thus the net cost to the taxpayer of paying a salary increment of 81.4 per cent would be reduced to 52.7 per cent.

Solution: let employees choose
The situation described so far is pretty bleak: an ever-increasing and seemingly irredeemable debt for future taxpayers. Meanwhile, by closing schemes, the private sector has failed to alleviate the burden of past costs but is, at least, starting to limit future costs.

What genuine solutions can there be, given the limited room for manoeuvre? There are two factors that surprisingly favour reform:

- *Tax:* the government effectively subsidises both private and public sector pensions through tax rebates. While this is a cost saving to the private sector employer, it is an extra cost to the government. It would be cheaper for the government to pay extra salary in cash than simply allow pension benefits of the same value to accrue.
- *Lack of understanding:* it could be argued that people do not make rational savings choices, and generally prefer short-term gains to long-term savings (see Pensions Commission,

2005, and also the response by Congdon, 2005, 2006 for an alternative view). This implies that, given the choice, people will choose a higher salary in cash over a pension. Even if people do fully understand the cost and benefits of their pension arrangements, they are unlikely to spend on pension percentages of their salary that are anywhere near as high as those indicated by Neil Record in Table 12.

An obvious solution is therefore to offer employees the choice of opting out of the schemes in return for a higher salary. This has many advantages:

- Unions cannot object, as there will be no change in the value of the existing benefits package. Indeed, they can have a positive role in educating the workforce as to the relative value of the pension against the salary alternative. Those who remained in schemes would have no change in their benefits package.
- Even if the salary alternative were generous, Table 19 shows that significant cost reductions can be achieved owing to the incidence of tax: those employees who chose the cash alternative would pay tax and National Insurance.
- The reform will make pension costs explicit and transparent.

Two further points are worth making. First, this proposed reform would not prevent simultaneous reform of public sector schemes. Indeed, if employees were given higher cash salaries and few employees wished to join the existing schemes given their costs, employers and employee representatives might wish to reform schemes to make them more attractive (see also the commentary by Philip Booth, above). Second, employees could, of course, join defined-contribution arrangements and contribute whatever percentage of their salary they wished. They would then obtain tax relief on contributions. Employees themselves must be better off because they could choose the amount of their pension provision and increase their cash salaries in return for giving up a compulsory benefit in kind. The salary and pension benefit may be of equal cost to the taxpayer but will have different subjective values to different public sector employees.

Conclusion

The current situation of spiralling costs and liabilities of public sector pension provision would have been wholly avoidable if the schemes had been funded and adequate governance structures had been put in place. Indeed, owing to the incidence of tax, the actual cost of the schemes to taxpayers, when expressed relative to salaries, is probably even higher than Neil Record's estimate.

As Neil Record has argued, the liabilities and the cost of accruing further liabilities should be made explicit: this would naturally follow from introducing a governance structure that already exists in the private sector.

Union intransigence, which is an inevitable result of the schemes' structures, has made the possibility of reform unlikely in the current climate. The extremely high cost of the schemes means, however, that employees can be offered generous extra salaries as inducements to voluntarily leave the schemes, avoiding the need for confrontation.

REFERENCES

Cardinale, M., G. Katz, J. Kumar and M. Orszag (2005), *Background Risk and Pensions*, London: Institute of Actuaries.

Congdon, T. (2005), 'The Pensions Commission: is Adair Turner irrational or confused?', *Economic Affairs*, 25(1): 56.

Congdon, T. (2006), 'On average, Britons out-think the Pensions Commission', *Economic Affairs*, 26(1): 70.

Haberman, S. and T. A. Sibbett (eds) (1995), *History of Actuarial Science*, London: Chatto and Pickering.

HMT (2000), *Review of Ill Health Retirement in the Public Sector*, London: HM Treasury.

HMT (2004), *Long-term Public Finance Report: an analysis of fiscal sustainability*, London: HM Treasury.

Pensions Commission (2005), *A New Pension Settlement for the Twenty-first Century: the second report of the Pensions Commission*, London: Stationery Office.

PPI (2005), *Occupational Pension Provision in the Public Sector*, London: Pensions Policy Institute.

Rhodes, G. (1965), *Public Sector Pensions*, London: George Allen and Unwin.

Sin, Y. (2001), *Administrative and Civil Service Reform: pension arrangements*, World Bank website,

UBS (2005), *Pension Fund Indicators 2005*, London: UBS Global Asset Management, London.

http://www1.worldbank.org/publicsector/civilservice/pension.htm.

ABOUT THE IEA

The Institute is a research and educational charity (No. CC 235 351), limited by guarantee. Its mission is to improve understanding of the fundamental institutions of a free society by analysing and expounding the role of markets in solving economic and social problems.

The IEA achieves its mission by:

- a high-quality publishing programme
- conferences, seminars, lectures and other events
- outreach to school and college students
- brokering media introductions and appearances

The IEA, which was established in 1955 by the late Sir Antony Fisher, is an educational charity, not a political organisation. It is independent of any political party or group and does not carry on activities intended to affect support for any political party or candidate in any election or referendum, or at any other time. It is financed by sales of publications, conference fees and voluntary donations.

In addition to its main series of publications the IEA also publishes a quarterly journal, *Economic Affairs*.

The IEA is aided in its work by a distinguished international Academic Advisory Council and an eminent panel of Honorary Fellows. Together with other academics, they review prospective IEA publications, their comments being passed on anonymously to authors. All IEA papers are therefore subject to the same rigorous independent refereeing process as used by leading academic journals.

IEA publications enjoy widespread classroom use and course adoptions in schools and universities. They are also sold throughout the world and often translated/reprinted.

Since 1974 the IEA has helped to create a world-wide network of 100 similar institutions in over 70 countries. They are all independent but share the IEA's mission.

Views expressed in the IEA's publications are those of the authors, not those of the Institute (which has no corporate view), its Managing Trustees, Academic Advisory Council members or senior staff.

Members of the Institute's Academic Advisory Council, Honorary Fellows, Trustees and Staff are listed on the following page.

The Institute gratefully acknowledges financial support for its publications programme and other work from a generous benefaction by the late Alec and Beryl Warren.

Other papers recently published by the IEA include:

WHO, What and Why?
Transnational Government, Legitimacy and the World Health Organization
Roger Scruton
Occasional Paper 113; ISBN 0 255 36487 3
£8.00

The World Turned Rightside Up
A New Trading Agenda for the Age of Globalisation
John C. Hulsman
Occasional Paper 114; ISBN 0 255 36495 4
£8.00

The Representation of Business in English Literature
Introduced and edited by Arthur Pollard
Readings 53; ISBN 0 255 36491 1
£12.00

Anti-Liberalism 2000
The Rise of New Millennium Collectivism
David Henderson
Occasional Paper 115; ISBN 0 255 36497 0
£7.50

Capitalism, Morality and Markets
Brian Griffiths, Robert A. Sirico, Norman Barry & Frank Field
Readings 54; ISBN 0 255 36496 2
£7.50

A Conversation with Harris and Seldon

Ralph Harris & Arthur Seldon
Occasional Paper 116; ISBN 0 255 36498 9
£7.50

Malaria and the DDT Story

Richard Tren & Roger Bate
Occasional Paper 117; ISBN 0 255 36499 7
£10.00

A Plea to Economists Who Favour Liberty:
Assist the Everyman

Daniel B. Klein
Occasional Paper 118; ISBN 0 255 36501 2
£10.00

The Changing Fortunes of Economic Liberalism

Yesterday, Today and Tomorrow
David Henderson
Occasional Paper 105 (new edition); ISBN 0 255 36520 9
£12.50

The Global Education Industry

Lessons from Private Education in Developing Countries
James Tooley
Hobart Paper 141 (new edition); ISBN 0 255 36503 9
£12.50

Saving Our Streams

The Role of the Anglers' Conservation Association in
Protecting English and Welsh Rivers
Roger Bate
Research Monograph 53; ISBN 0 255 36494 6
£10.00

Better Off Out?

The Benefits or Costs of EU Membership
Brian Hindley & Martin Howe
Occasional Paper 99 (new edition); ISBN 0 255 36502 0
£10.00

Buckingham at 25

Freeing the Universities from State Control
Edited by James Tooley
Readings 55; ISBN 0 255 36512 8
£15.00

Lectures on Regulatory and Competition Policy

Irwin M. Stelzer
Occasional Paper 120; ISBN 0 255 36511 X
£12.50

Misguided Virtue

False Notions of Corporate Social Responsibility
David Henderson
Hobart Paper 142; ISBN 0 255 36510 1
£12.50

HIV and Aids in Schools

The Political Economy of Pressure Groups and Miseducation
Barrie Craven, Pauline Dixon, Gordon Stewart & James Tooley
Occasional Paper 121; ISBN 0 255 36522 5
£10.00

The Road to Serfdom

The Reader's Digest *condensed version*
Friedrich A. Hayek
Occasional Paper 122; ISBN 0 255 36530 6
£7.50

Bastiat's *The Law*

Introduction by Norman Barry
Occasional Paper 123; ISBN 0 255 36509 8
£7.50

A Globalist Manifesto for Public Policy

Charles Calomiris
Occasional Paper 124; ISBN 0 255 36525 X
£7.50

Euthanasia for Death Duties

Putting Inheritance Tax Out of Its Misery
Barry Bracewell-Milnes
Research Monograph 54; ISBN 0 255 36513 6
£10.00

Liberating the Land
The Case for Private Land-use Planning
Mark Pennington
Hobart Paper 143; ISBN 0 255 36508 x
£10.00

IEA Yearbook of Government Performance 2002/2003
Edited by Peter Warburton
Yearbook 1; ISBN 0 255 36532 2
£15.00

Britain's Relative Economic Performance, 1870–1999
Nicholas Crafts
Research Monograph 55; ISBN 0 255 36524 1
£10.00

Should We Have Faith in Central Banks?
Otmar Issing
Occasional Paper 125; ISBN 0 255 36528 4
£7.50

The Dilemma of Democracy
Arthur Seldon
Hobart Paper 136 (reissue); ISBN 0 255 36536 5
£10.00

Fifty Economic Fallacies Exposed
Geoffrey E. Wood
Occasional Paper 129; ISBN 0 255 36518 7
£12.50

A Market in Airport Slots
Keith Boyfield (editor), David Starkie, Tom Bass & Barry Humphreys
Readings 56; ISBN 0 255 36505 5
£10.00

Money, Inflation and the Constitutional Position of the Central Bank
Milton Friedman & Charles A. E. Goodhart
Readings 57; ISBN 0 255 36538 1
£10.00

railway.com
Parallels between the Early British Railways and the ICT Revolution
Robert C. B. Miller
Research Monograph 57; ISBN 0 255 36534 9
£12.50

The Regulation of Financial Markets
Edited by Philip Booth & David Currie
Readings 58; ISBN 0 255 36551 9
£12.50

Climate Alarmism Reconsidered
Robert L. Bradley Jr
Hobart Paper 146; ISBN 0 255 36541 1
£12.50

Government Failure: E. G. West on Education
Edited by James Tooley & James Stanfield
Occasional Paper 130; ISBN 0 255 36552 7
£12.50

Waging the War of Ideas
John Blundell
Second edition
Occasional Paper 131; ISBN 0 255 36547 0
£12.50

Corporate Governance: Accountability in the Marketplace
Elaine Sternberg
Second edition
Hobart Paper 147; ISBN 0 255 36542 X
£12.50

The Land Use Planning System
Evaluating Options for Reform
John Corkindale
Hobart Paper 148; ISBN 0 255 36550 0
£10.00

Economy and Virtue
Essays on the Theme of Markets and Morality
Edited by Dennis O'Keeffe
Readings 59; ISBN 0 255 36504 7
£12.50

Free Markets Under Siege

Cartels, Politics and Social Welfare
Richard A. Epstein
Occasional Paper 132; ISBN 0 255 36553 5
£10.00

Unshackling Accountants

D. R. Myddelton
Hobart Paper 149; ISBN 0 255 36559 4
£12.50

The Euro as Politics

Pedro Schwartz
Research Monograph 58; ISBN 0 255 36535 7
£12.50

Pricing Our Roads

Vision and Reality
Stephen Glaister & Daniel J. Graham
Research Monograph 59; ISBN 0 255 36562 4
£10.00

The Role of Business in the Modern World

Progress, Pressures, and Prospects for the Market Economy
David Henderson
Hobart Paper 150; ISBN 0 255 36548 9
£12.50

Public Service Broadcasting Without the BBC?

Alan Peacock
Occasional Paper 133; ISBN 0 255 36565 9
£10.00

The ECB and the Euro: the First Five Years

Otmar Issing

Occasional Paper 134; ISBN 0 255 36555 1

£10.00

Towards a Liberal Utopia?

Edited by Philip Booth

Hobart Paperback 32; ISBN 0 255 36563 2

£15.00

The Way Out of the Pensions Quagmire

Philip Booth & Deborah Cooper

Research Monograph 60; ISBN 0 255 36517 9

£12.50

Black Wednesday

A Re-examination of Britain's Experience in the Exchange Rate Mechanism

Alan Budd

Occasional Paper 135; ISBN 0 255 36566 7

£7.50

Crime: Economic Incentives and Social Networks

Paul Ormerod

Hobart Paper 151; ISBN 0 255 36554 3

£10.00

The Road to Serfdom *with* The Intellectuals and Socialism

Friedrich A. Hayek

Occasional Paper 136; ISBN 0 255 36576 4

£10.00

Money and Asset Prices in Boom and Bust

Tim Congdon
Hobart Paper 152; ISBN 0 255 36570 5
£10.00

The Dangers of Bus Re-regulation

and Other Perspectives on Markets in Transport
John Hibbs et al.
Occasional Paper 137; ISBN 0 255 36572 1
£10.00

The New Rural Economy

Change, Dynamism and Government Policy
Berkeley Hill et al.
Occasional Paper 138; ISBN 0 255 36546 2
£15.00

The Benefits of Tax Competition

Richard Teather
Hobart Paper 153; ISBN 0 255 36569 1
£12.50

Wheels of Fortune

Self-funding Infrastructure and the Free Market Case for a Land Tax
Fred Harrison
Hobart Paper 154; ISBN 0 255 36589 6
£12.50

Were 364 Economists All Wrong?

Edited by Philip Booth
Readings 60
ISBN-10: 0 255 36588 8; ISBN-13: 978 0 255 36588 8
£10.00

Europe After the 'No' Votes

Mapping a New Economic Path
Patrick A. Messerlin
Occasional Paper 139
ISBN-10: 0 255 36580 2; ISBN-13: 978 0 255 36580 2
£10.00

The Railways, the Market and the Government

John Hibbs et al.
Readings 61
ISBN-10: 0 255 36567 5; ISBN-13: 978 0 255 36567 3
£12.50

Choice and the End of Social Housing

Peter King
Hobart Paper 155
ISBN-10: 0 255 36568 3; ISBN-13: 978 0 255 36568 0
£10.00

To order copies of currently available IEA papers, or to enquire about availability, please contact:

Gazelle
IEA orders
FREEPOST RLYS-EAHU-YSCZ
White Cross Mills
Hightown
Lancaster LA1 4XS

Tel: 01524 68765
Fax: 01524 63232
Email: sales@gazellebooks.co.uk

The IEA also offers a subscription service to its publications. For a single annual payment, currently £40.00 in the UK, you will receive every monograph the IEA publishes during the course of a year and discounts on our extensive back catalogue. For more information, please contact:

Adam Myers
Subscriptions
The Institute of Economic Affairs
2 Lord North Street
London SW1P 3LB

Tel: 020 7799 8920
Fax: 020 7799 2137
Website: www.iea.org.uk